A WRITER IS A STATE OF BEING

Bob Zimmer: Now that I know your name, I'll not forget it. I'll be watching for it in the papers. and the booklists. Sue

Also by Susan Henry

ESKIMO LEGENDS a primary grade reader

ACTIVITIES FOR ALASKA KINDERGARTENS AND FIRST GRADES co-authored by Terry Sloat

ECHOES OF THE PAST an anthology of Yup'ik Eskimo tales

I WANT A DOBERMAN BY MY DESK the other stuff you learn at school

A WRITER IS A STATE OF BEING

YOUR PERSONAL DESKTOP CONFERENCE

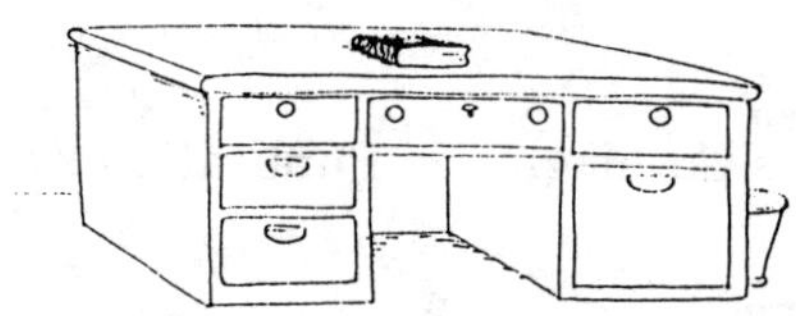

Susan Henry

RICKREALL CREEK HOUSE

 Published by Rickreall Creek House, Box 13, Rickreall, Oregon 97371. (503) 623-6889, SAN 668-1166.

Printed in United States of America. Published simultaneously in Rickreall, Oregon; Ilwaco, Washington; Mountain Village, Alaska; and basement offices and dining room tabletops wherever writers congregate alone.

Typography and design by Kerri Hunter, Salem, Oregon.

Art by Jack Corbett

Library of Congress Cataloging in Publication 87-51002

ISBN 0-943149-05-3

To Mrs. Handel, Miss Buchurench, and Dr. Sorvig,
who said I couldn't;

To Emit Boyd, Miriam Chapman, and G. Russell Ross,
who thought I could;

To Tom Ferte and Art Williams, who weren't
surprised when I did;

And especially to Bob,
who let me do it.

I've written for an employer; I've been a reporter and a freelancer. I've published commercially and have self-published. The best steady potboiler income has been journalism; the most artistic satisfaction is self-publishing.

Artists I know who sell their work all over the country just load up their car with their work and start out, stopping at all the galleries along the way. I expect authors do the same with their books.

Artist, gallery owner

CONTENTS

APPENDIX: CONFERNCE DISPLAY AREA

SAMPLES AND ILLUSTRATIONS

YOUR PERSONAL DESKTOP CONFERENCE

GENERAL SESSION

Welcome

Keynote

Susan Henry
2519 E. Ellendale
Dallas, OR 97338
(503) 623-6889

Approx 750 words
First Rights

PART I: GENERAL SESSION

WELCOME

By Susan Henry

Welcome to your own personal desktop conference.

It's personal because it's yours, whether you are a poet, freelancer, author, writer, or journalist--each has its own identity and all have some identicalnesses.

It's a conference because here are convened scores of writers, editors, agents, publishers. Together they bring a millenium of experience: the conflicts of time, space and family; the pain of rejections and the dues-paying internship of writing-for-free; the labor and uncertainty of being a novice; the glow and wonderment of success--and how it was attained. They come to share.

You can attend this conference on your own terms, on your own schedule, in your own place. You can attend whichever sessions you wish, or skip out unnoticed. You can attend in your pajamas if you want--and why not; a lot of it was written in pajamas.

Written, yes. As you already can tell, this conference is a book. The written form, after all, is a fairly appropriate mode of addressing writers. It's a book 8½ by 11 because that's writers' **size**, and portions are formatted in writers' style. It's supposed to be a visual aid.

This very text, for instance, is written in manuscript format; a detailed explanation appears in our Conference Display Area. Likewise, Sample Query Letters, Article Proposals, Letter to a Resource Person, and Cover Letter to Accompany a Manuscript appear in typed format. As fiction writers know, "Show, don't tell."

Throughout this conference, I have called upon and quoted many persons representing many segments of the

(more)

literary community. Sources are credited whenever the speakers spoke in print, in conferences, groups, or personally and as a matter of record. Many quotes are not credited, however; many ideas and opinions were personal confidences served with coffee. A guiding principle of journalism which I just made up is that one is more likely to speak candidly if the journalist is less likely to identify the speaker.

And, well, the fact is some of the ideas and inspirations of this conference are my own. It's some kind of literary license of conference facilitators. Although I'm not a writer of longstanding nor one of recognition as are most guest speakers appearing here, that may present certain advantages. I think that too often, "old" writers get to be like professors of education: too long out of the classroom, and they forget how it is in the real world. Or perhaps that how it was then isn't like it is now. "Old" writers tell "new" writers how easy it is to break in, how simple to write a dazzling query destined for acceptance, how quickly one writes his way into the highest-paying markets, how the formulas are fool-proof, and how all you need to succeed is determination. This conference doesn't say those things because for most of them it just isn't that way.

(more)

Nor is this one of those "everything you want to know about" tomes. I couldn't know what you want to know, and I do not write gospels. (But then, I'm hearing there's some doubt as to who did, in fact, write The Gospels. See, there are no absolutes.) I relate what I have found to be real, useful, and workable for me; other writers appearing here tell what is real for them. Together, we convey the basics and the protocols that are fundamental to all.

Beyond the basics, though, it's like making a Saturday soup: You throw in the ingredients you have around. As chefs and as writers, we don't always agree upon what constitutes a good cook, or a good book. Your creative ingredients--your theme, topic, form, content, style, terminologies--are your own, not found in equal measure in anyone else's stew. Your own unique flavor.

The majority of proper nouns in this book are of the Pacific Northwest because I am of the Northwest and that's my familiar ground. While the basics and the protocols are generally applicable anywhere, I don't happen to know many people elsewhere; and one of the primo principles of non-fiction is that the writer should hang in with what he knows or can verify. So I have sought out persons I know, where they live; but I

(more)

hope writers in Minnesota, Maine, Gulf Coast City, and in town and counties all over The Land of the Freelancer will come to our conference, too.

I hope this conference proves worthwhile. So worthwhile that Your Personal Desktop Conference is given a long-term place in the clutter on your desktop, and not in the circular file beside it.

##########

Keynote

A WRITER IS A STATE OF BEING

Why do writers write?

Because they have to.

Some say it's a psychobiochemicalelectrical program they're born with, maybe even contained in a strange extra chromosome: the need to write is part of writers' psychology and physiology as surely as the need for food, sleep, acceptance, and moving around from place to place.

A writer is perceptive, creative, obsessed, possessed.

A writer is a state of being.

Are writers "funny", too?

"Wacky as hell," says Thomas Ferte, poet and teacher who's been around the writers' circuit for a quarter-century, and who knows a lot of them. "The craziest are poets, followed by novelists, playwrights, short story writers, and then non- fictionalists and journalists."

Tim Hinshaw, Salem writer-editor-publisher, agrees he and his pen friends are funny, and he agrees poets are the funniest. He places journalists next, though. And, says Hinshaw, even when journalists turn over a new leaf, they just go from Funny One to Funny Two.

Proving it, he says, "When I started out in the early Seventies, journalists banged typewriters and drank. Then they changed to computers and became sprout eaters."

"Being funny goes along with perceptiveness, and with creativity," says Ferte.

But being creative isn't enough. A decent writer must be a technician of the language, whatever his language. A writer must acquire mastery of the elements of grammar, structure, and cadance, as surely as a musician must master notation, fingering and phrasing.

A writer must be a severe self-critic. "Edit ruthlessly," is how the editor of a national magazine phrases it. "An artist throws out 85% of what he produces," Dr. Laurence Lyon, professor of musical composition at Western Oregon State College tells his students. Remember that. (The trash barrel in my office is larger than the one in my kitchen.) And you can't be a critic unless you've mastered those technical rudiments.

Must a writer write to be a writer? Of course, insist those who scoff the going-to-be writers. Every day. Not so, say others. A writer, say they, is an inspiration, an attitude: An aspirer who has not yet set out is still a writer in nature and spirit and that genetic mutation and in state of going-to-be being. Most of us are "going to be" years before we "are"; and if that strange chromosome is the cause of our obsession, are the going-to-be's not also of the writer's persuasion?

If you are programmed to be, you probably will work on it.

When? When do you write?

Early. Some, like Oregon's poet laureate William Stafford, arise at 5 a.m. "When I was in the military, I worked for myself every day before I went to work for Uncle," he told a writers' class.

Late. "I seldom begin before 9 a.m.," says Marsha Weber; and thousands of others work into the night. "Don't call me after 3 a.m.," says Marje Blood; that's when Sharon Wood quits working and goes out shopping.

But the real world is too much with us, early and late. We must go forth daily to the real world of work, of nurturing children, mowing the lawn, cleaning the garage, entertaining laws, in-laws, and business associates. Finding the time to write is one of our greatest difficulties, almost as hard as finding a place to do it.

Designate in your home a room for an office, say the writers' advisories. A room with a door, which, when closed, announces to all who share your dwellingplace that door shall be neither knockethed on nor entered. Well, whence cometh this room? Which child shall be evicted? Dare you establish an office in same room as sleeping spouse? While you click and clack, early and late?

Children and spouse: an inseparable part of your state of being, for few wo/men are islands. To many, families present the greatest frustration. Mickey Hickman, author of *Homer, the Country Boy*, said his wife "barely tolerates" his writing life - and he said this even as he was negotiating movie rights. The truth is that many families tolerate barely, some not at all. Because, as we already established, writers become obsessed, "funny".

First, forget the children's opinions. They'll grow up and leave home. They'll soon enough nurture their own obsessions, and then they'll understand yours. If they don't, don't worry about it. Don't worry about what your parents think, either.

That leaves only your spouse's feelings as a point of significant concern. Spouses often fail to understand why one chooses not to go places and do things, how one can allow the lawn to grow long and die down, how making a poem can be a greater desire than making out. Many spouses, most spouses, come around after the first couple of published bylines and a check. Some never do.

For persons whose program commands them to write and who meet resistance on the homefront, the options are obvious. And accurate. One can compose as one can, a few lines or a paragraph a week; or abandon writing altogether; or await retirement, widowhood, or become unmarried. Tens of thousands begin their writing after retirement; writing classes at senior centers and elderhostels are packed. And, understandably perhaps, other thousands become single. That's a fact of the state of being. Maybe that's what Willamette Writers mean: "Writing is the world's loneliest profession."

In *Holy the Firm* Annie Dillard says, in effect, that if you want to write seriously, you have to take a broadax to your life. Funny, wacky, lonely . . . broadaxed. We are.

A writer who writes is motivated. One who continues writing is disciplined. He is also persevering and thick-skinned. He has to be to weather rejections and, when his work is published, to withstand with grace the changes, deletions, and rearrangement of the words he so carefully birthed and nutured.

The typical writer is not richly rewarded in the financial sense. Hundreds of books, hundreds more presenters of classes, conferences, and workshops promise you can earn big bucks. A local community college instructor told his aspiring freelancers they should expect to recieve from $500 to $1500 for an article. "I do, you should," he promised. You can check out the accuracy of his claim with a quick scan of *Writer's Market*. A presenter of seminars in a coastal state titles his presentations "How to Sell 75% of What You Write." For $195 he'll tell you to query first, then write the piece after your go-ahead.

Such promises are cruel carrots dangled before hopeful authors for the purpose of selling books, workshops, or, as in the instructor's case, self-serving an ego. The big bucks are in someone else's seminars, not in your creativity.

The real figures disclaim the big-bucks assurances. According to a publisher's trade paper, only 5% of American writers earn more than $5000 per year as writers. Fewer than 4% earn their living from writing. Thousands who call themselves professional writers also hold full-time jobs to pay the bills. "A good writer has no reason to be surprised when the world offers him less in the way of fame and riches than he deserves," writes Susan Lardner in The *New Yorker,* Nov. 23, 1987.

If you love to write--translation "have to"--none of this will cure you nor scare you off. Some people golf, some watch movies, some write. And, anyway, writers reap considerable rewards not financial. When a product of your creativity is accepted for publication, the editor is saying,

"What you say is valid and valuable, and worth sharing."

Today, the written word is no less influential than it was before the time of high-tech information and entertainment. Every drama, every commercial, every lyric, news item, Supreme Court decision, product label, owner's manual, course description, every memo, song, sign, speech, no matter how performed, presented, or transmitted, is first set down in written form. The pen has lost none of its power. It's still the writers of the world who fashion the words--written, sung, displayed, or spoken.

A writer is a being who provides our social order, the individuals and the collective that constitute our populace, with entertainment--that psychological release that allows one to retain or regain balance; with information and inspiration; and with the seeds to grow new ideas, the perspectives that conceive and institute actions and progress.

You can't take those kinds of rewards to the bank.

A writer is what he is and he can't help it. So be.

"Be a writer...and teach us how to LIVE."--David Morgan

SESSION 1

BEGINNING TO BE

What Does a Writer Need?

How Do You Learn to Write?

Ideas and Writer's Block

Knocking the Outrageous

THE BASICS:

WHAT DOES A WRITER REALLY NEED?

"The people who get rooked into spending too much on stuff they don't need are primary-grade teachers and writers," said an elementary principal whose spouse is a teacher and a writer.

It comes from dedication, a zeal to do it better, and an awful time crunch that makes them willing to pay for shortcuts, self- improvement, and information.

Too many of those expenditures for professionalism are unnecessaary. Too often, the goods purchased are not useful, the information inapplicable.

For a writer, the difference between solvency and loss is only a few bucks - one more item sold and one less bought. To IRS, the difference between being a professional and a hobbyist is whether income exceeds expenses for three of five years. So! . . . If you don't need it, don't buy it. Not at the outset.

A starting-out writer needs only the bony necessities; invest in supplementary supplies and services later, gradually, under a long-range business plan. Then expand as you're able to capitalize.

THE ABSOLUTE NECESSITIES

Automatic writing machine

Option A: Typewriter. Needs 10-pitch (spaces per inch) spacing cabability with a clear, unembellished typeface.

Necessary typewriter ancillaries: Clear black ribbon. Don't send queries and submissions from gray-toned ribbon; only shades of black will do.

Correction tape for original-copy submissions. "Liquid Secretary" or "boo-boo-goo" can be fine for photocopy work IF it doesn't smudge the ink it's supposed to cover, or create valleys, canyons, or shadows on the page.

Backing sheet. That's the second sheet, the empty page placed in back of the paper being typed upon. Using a backing results in clearer, darker type; and the cushioning gives your platen years of added life. You can reuse the same backing sheet multiple times, but don't type on it later; it's pocked with key impressions.

Option B: Word processor/computer. Must be able to print in 10 or 12 characters per inch; editors won't bother trying to read smaller. Many editors won't accept dot matrix hard copy, so you need a near-letter-quality printer.

If you're a starting-out writer without a word processor, don't rush out to buy one right away. Writers who use WP's claim they at least double their output with the help of their hi-tek tools, and after working at the Kaypro + Wordstar down at the newspaper, I know it's true. But. If you don't now own one, you should first be sure you have marketable output to put out (publishable work) before investing in hard and software.

Paper - White, unlined, 50# or 60#, 8-1/2 x 11". Never use erasable.

You can, of course, compose notes and drafts on anything. You can probably find reams, literally, of free-for-the-taking discards from photocopy centers. Print shops are another source of inexpensive draft paper. If you photocopy finished manuscripts, you can type them on photocopy paper, which is less expensive than high-quality bond. And writers who have the knack of composing at the computer need paper only for final, printed- out hard copy.

#10 envelopes - Business-size

6 x 9 envelopes - For manuscript/cover letter/photo/art packages exceeding four pages.

Dictionary

Thesaurus

Writer's Market - LATEST edition. Bookstores.

Writers Northwest Handbook - Latest edition. For markets in Montana, Washington, Oregon, Idaho, Alaska, British Columbia. Bookstores or from Media Weavers, Rt. 3 Box 376, Hillsboro, OR 97214. $12.95 + $1.50 p&h.

File folders

Record keeping system - For queries, responses; submissions -- what to where, when, results; expenditures and receipts; information, clippings, ideas, resources. Filing cabinets are wonderful, and one lends a classy, prosperous appearance to your office. Filing cabinets are also pretty pricey and an el-cheapo is a waste of funds. Until your work generates a cash flow, a Monarch Rum carton will exactly hold your file folders.

ENHANCERS

Letterhead stationery - For queries, professional correspondence. NOT for manuscripts.

Matching envelopes enhance your professional appearance.

World Almanac - Up-to-date names, addresses, figures, facts for article development; resource person contacts; lists of organizations; toll-free telephone numbers.

Sourcebook for contacts -- *Directory of Experts, Authorities, and Spokespersons: the Talk Show Guest Directory.* Mitchell P. Davis, Editor. From Broadcast Interview Source, 2500 Wisconsin Ave. N.W., Washington, D.C. 20007-4570. $25.

Writer's organization membership - For support, networking, resource people, updated markets, how-to. Most established associations publish newsletters which themselves are worth the membership fee. Many also sponsor workshops and conferences, often in the "fairly pricey" range.

BUY SOME BUT CHOOSE CAREFULLY

Conference, Courses, Seminars, Workshops -- Dozens of How to Write and How to Sell books and magazines swamp the market. What they do, says our principal friend, is to "prey on struggling writers' ambitions". What they also do is to present the same topics and the same information, over and over.

If you select two or three appropriate conferences and courses, and if you read and heed advice and how-to found in *Writer's Market* and *Writers Northwest Handbook*, you'll have most of what you need for two or three years. Most else is mere repetition.

Instead of subscribing to the writers' mags, flip through issues on the newsstand or at the library. If you find something you need, then buy that issue. You will find many worthwhile books at the library, on all aspects of the craft.

Manuscript critique services - The magazines and newsletters are full of ads for these. Fees vary, and so do the credentials of editors and critics. Many critics charge more for reading than you'll sell the manuscript for. On the other hand, a reliable, professional critic can provide you with comments and insights on one manuscript which will give you an overall assessment of your total skills and techniques, and which you can apply to all your writing.

You often can get your work critiqued for the price of the deal at writers' groups and college classes.

Frugality is an attribute. If you err, let it be on the side of austerity. But. There's a point where frugal becomes stingy and being a tightwad stands in the way of progress. Like the freelancer who says, "I'll just use the library's *Writer's Market."* Or like me, who had chronic neck-and-shoulder pain for three years: When I bought a $10.95 copyholder, it went away.

Every craftsman needs the right tools for the job. Just be sure the tools you get are ones you need.

There are two universal protocols of the publishing industry. One is SASE: Self-Addressed Stamped Envelope. Every query, submission, question, or request for information must be accompanied by a postpaid envelope addressed to yourself. The other is that any item you send anyone which you intend for publication must be typed (or computer-printed) and double-spaced. A writer who fails to observe both of these points will not be taken seriously as a professional.

HOW DO YOU LEARN TO WRITE?

Nobody is born knowing how to write right, acquisitions agent David Morgan told a Willamette Writers Conference. Writing is a set of rules and skills which must be learned, and to learn a skill one must study and practice.

> No person was born knowing how to write well; writing is a skill one has to
> LEARN...
> Don't say you can't.
> Start practising.
> --DAVID MORGAN

Where to learn? Well, how about back there in the grades--why do you think it's called grammar school? Writers must know the rules of grammar and their applications in the technical aspects of the written language.

Nouns, verbs, subjects, modifiers, infinitives, participles, transitions, sequence, subtopics. Punctuation. Spelling.

"And you won't learn to write by majoring in English," said one who regretted her choice of degree. In fact some colleges don't even offer courses in grammar; others, one class once yearly.

Don't worry about whether
you have talent;
as soon as you
start to worry,
you negate the possibility
of having it...

There are plenty of grammar manuals and usage handbooks, and owning one is a good idea. But they're for review, refreshing, and reference more than for instruction. What to do? If you need basic instruction, go to your nearest community college center.

Theirs is the most thorough, time-efficient and cost-effective basic skills course. (This is euphamism for high school bonehead English; and if you didn't get it then, it will be painful now, too. Do it.)

How, after the mechanics, do you learn to write?

...Not everyone makes it
as a writer--only
those
who
try.
DAVID MORGAN

Read. Not for escape and entertainment but to study. To dissect, analyze, evaluate. Since one of my bags is journalism, I read papers, particularly those town weeklies and neighborhood news types. And believe it, a lot of the "small" papers have some mighty fine writers, warmer, more caring and empathetic, more creative, more literary than USA Today reporters whose deadline dictates they don't have time. I read papers to study structure, style, tone, persona.

When you read, identify what you like and why: how is the writing effective? I study George Will for his crisp, snappy style, barbed but not abusive. I study Ellen Goodman for her brillant use of words, phrases, and flow; she lends literary treatment to social and political commentary. I study Art Buchwald because *that's* how to write humor.

There are three books I consider my finest study materials.

Country Chaff II by Jerry Easterling. West Side Publishing Company, 1988. ISBN 0-944540-03-1, $6.95. Easterling is a sensory writer. You see, hear, feel, and experience. He puts a precise word in the precise phrase so that one feels the warmth and moves with the cadance. His writing is a tone poem.

Jam on the Ceiling by J. Wesley Sullivan. Navillus, 1987. ISBN 0-9618152-0-5. $6.95. Sullivan is eclectic. He demonstrates equally exemplary styles as a humorist and as an analyst of current affairs. His range includes Cosby-like guffaw, Buchwaldian subtle tickelry, and George Willy crisp, informed commentary.

East is West of Here by Joyce Thompson. Breitenbush, 1987. ISBN 0-932576-32-X. $15. From Thompson I learned more about structure and quality of short fiction than in any five-credit class. If you do short stories, please study this one. If you don't write fiction, study it anyway, for its structure and style. Thompson does things with sentences and punctuation that, if you study her, will make YOU a better writer.

Notice: None of these is a product of a New York "big house." All are Northwest authors, Grand Ronde, Salem, Seattle; all are Northwest small presses, Salem, Corvallis, Portland. You needn't be dazzled by the big time.

So let's talk about the big time. So many writers and critics speak of the poor literary qualities of best-seller novels from "major houses" that I decided to read one. A rarity. From a store dealing in previously read books I selected a Danielle Steel, reasoning that if I were going for trash it may as well be best-selling stuff; like is there fine trash and flop stuff? Steel's *Full Circle* is indeed full . . . of inconsistencies in characterizations, unexplained miracle cures for their psychoses, quirks, and hang-ups; structural errors, syntax out of synch. In some brief shining passages literary craftsmanship was obviously attempted either by writer or an editor; but it's so out of Steel's style that it only comes off as ludicrous, a parody of itself. Still, Steel is a worthwhile study.

The other kind of studious reading you must do is of the periodicals you hope to contribute to. And once you analyze a style, you may decide it's not yours. "Write what you want," says M. K. Wren, "and if a publication's style isn't yours, don't write it. Unless you want to."

Edit. Practice your skills by editing material in print. Compose a different lead. Select a different word to make a meaning more precise, an effect more powerful. Turn a phrase differently. Improve sentence structure, sentence combining, sentence variety. Is this being critical? Well, certainly; just as critical as an editor will be with your work.

Good copy to practice editing: Locally-written "colyums" in hometown weeklies; confessions and romance mags; letters to the editor (almost certainly edited already); newsletters; best- sellers; Safeway's weekly ads.

Write. Writers learn to write by writing.

Write regularly and steadily. "Fifteen uninterrupted minutes a day," advises Henriette Klauser (*Writing on Both Sides of the Brain*). "If you do it first thing in the morning, your subconscius will process it throughout the day." If your composing is done late in the day, though, says Joyce Thompson, it will be processed during REM sleep, and once entered there, it's likely to become a part of you.

> If poets are the sprinters of literature, novelists are the marathoners. And all need to keep fit through daily practice.
> JOYCE THOMPSON

Rewrite. Rewrite what someone else has written, making it fit your own mode. Use material you've edited and, retaining its substance, compose it all over from scratch, this time in your own style.

Rewrite what you have written, this time reversing the intent: Make your writing fit the style of someone else you'd like to write for.

And keep writing. Here's fair warning: Use it or lose it.

Athletes lose 20% of their power every day they do not work out; the same is true of our muscle tone and aerobic capacity. G. Russell Ross, my brass instructor at Central Washington State College (now CWSU) told us that wind instrumentalists' embouchure and ability declined by 20% every day we neglected to practice. Wayne Hertz preached the same doctrine to his vocal students. (When I was in college, I thought God's name was Mr. Hertz.)

Do you think readers and writers lose it, too? Let me tell you, from my years as a teacher I know it's so. I knew what kids could do in June, and I saw what the same kids did in late August. It took them until October to regain it.

How do you learn to write? Learn the rules. Read. Edit. Write and rewrite. Learning, yes; all these are forms of scholarship. And if a professional writer is not a scholar, who is?

As David Morgan put it, "Every writer continues learning, no matter how accomplished he becomes."

> Writers are like pilot lights
> waiting to be turned on.
> When an idea is fanned on...
> VOOM!
> HENRIETTE KLAUSER

IDEAS AND WRITER'S BLOCK

Two of the most often-asked questions: Don't you ever have writer's block? Where do you get your ideas?

They're related questions. Because frequently the question is phrased: "When you sit down to write, are you ever without ideas?"

You don't just sit down to write, waiting for ideas. An idea is the end, not the start of the thought process.

First, stimuli: the sights, sounds, experiences around you.

Next, perceptions: awareness of those surroundings. As teachers say, "The stuff's there; I have to get your attention."

Then, processing: categorizing, classifying, filing incoming information in the correct mental compartments.

Then, recalling, analyzing: retrieving what's filed, taking it out, examining.

Finally, collating diverse bits of information and, with both sides of the brain, creating an idea.

A writer is an idea person. With experience, perception, and practice, ideas will start chasing you around with ever- accelerating speed and profusion until soon it becomes necessary to jot down words, phrases, lists, references, to keep track of them all. Robert M. Pyle, many-books author and instructor at Grays Harbor College, tells his students, "Don't squander your observations in the dimensions of your memory--write them down!"

Writers would rather WRITE; but we also have to perform all those mundanities of life. Ideas? The next story grows while we do those things we have to do but wish we weren't doing because we'd rather be writing about it than doing it.

It's like this. When we bought the farm, the whole estate had turned into a blackberry patch. While I labored to eradicate those beastly briars, I also formulated to the last detail and word "Parable of the Blackberries."

A story about the blackberry story. Shortly after the magazine arrived it was plopped on the sofa, opened to the page. When Bob walked into the room, he spotted the title, lettered in big, bold calligraphy. "Is that yours?" he asked.

"What makes you think so?"

"I can spot your stuff clear across the room."

The piece was intended to be one of those heavy messages delivered in a light tone. In phrases such as "it came to pass" and "and in this wise", it was a gentle parody, you see. When I read it to Bob, we both got sore sides; it came across as pure beef baloney.

"It's sure amazing how different the stuff looks in print," I marveled.

While teaching high school I planned and chaperoned many student trips, developing an efficient, goof-proof pre-travel things-to-do list and a schedule for doing them. Once a principal whose students had disasterfied a school trip sighed, "I wish someone would make up a check-list that would organize kids and teachers." My background and experience, plus a chance remark, resulted in *Music Educators Journal's* "Checklist for Student Travel."

From scraps of sociology, history, and psychology gathered over the years, I concluded that most religions recognize reincarnation; and also that in some ancient societies cats were sacred. And we have a cat with a mighty royal attitude whom I suspect tries to hustle my husband. Some facts, some fantasy, and I had a story about a reincarnated cat who had hot paws for its owner, led him into a fatal ambush, and got him recycled as its new feline mate. Naturally the story was composed while I killed blackberries.

I have a huge garden because farms are supposed to have gardens; but I'd rather be writing. So I asked other gardeners for their easy-labor tricks. It became "Gardening: Lightening the Labor" for *Gurney's Gardening News*. When my zucchini vines headed for the highway, Bob said, "Your zukes are going to take over Oregon." His remark turned into twice-published "How Oregon Got Squashed."

And so on. You get the idea about getting ideas and about turning out the piece while you turn out your chores.

Whether germinating story ideas or composing the words, many writers think and drive. Salem forester Mickey Bellman's job keeps him on the road for 200 miles at a clatter, so he organizes and composes as he drives. He says he seldom has writer's block because he has his material virtually written before he begins writing.

William Linville of Dallas is an active freelancer who's also a thinking driver. His tape recorder occupies his passenger seat, and it collects all those zippy ideas, snappy phrases, and grabby openers that hit him while he's at the wheel.

According to editors we polled, 90 to 95% of queries are rejected; of the queries getting editorial go-ahead, half the resulting completed articles are rejected.

Editors are starving for copy.
If you have good ideas
and write well,
you'll sell.

SUSAN STANLEY

About half of writer's block comes before the first sentence. A good lead, good enough to use in your query, and your piece practically writes itself from there, says Thomas Bannan, a Monmouth freelancer who's supported himself that way for 17 years. (Tom's a farmer, too; see, there's one born every day.) The words for that great, grabby beginning can be composed while you do those other things you have to do before you start writing.

Another time we block out is when we're shopping for that precise, exact word--usually the word that was in the recall file a minute ago. Instead of stopping to agonize, leave a blank and go on. That elusive word will return, say at four in the morning.

It may surprise you to realize the extent to which you already write while you work. "I was so glad the garden was gone for the year," says Vancouver novelist Sunni Sinjem, "until I realized that's where I'd been writing the chapters."

KNOCKING THE OUTRAGEOUS

At a workshop I presented, a participant commented, disdainfully, I think, "It seems like you knock writers' magazines." It's not any magazine I knock, but some of their outrageous advice.

In order to sell, a magazine has to present a new, catchy, different perspective. A writer may have to come off the wall to sell to the magazine; the magazine may have to be outrageous to sell to the readers. A point to keep in mind when you, yourself, propose to create copy that sells.

The most incredibly irrational advice, but advice published with fair regularity, is that soon after you've sold your third or fourth piece, you should chuck the old 8-to-5 with its fringies and retirement plan and go to work as a full-time self - employed writer.

Before you resign, resign yourself to the statistics.

According to editors we polled, 90 to 95% of queries are rejected; of the queries getting editorial go-ahead, half the resulting completed articles are rejected.

According to a leading West Coast literary agent, 98% of all book proposals are turned down.

> The self-employed writers of America number 14,000 full-timers and 47,000 part-timers, reports biographer Kitty Kelley in August 24, 1987 *Newsweek*. This does not include those who write for an employer, such as journalists, technical writers, and others whose writing is part of their employment.

Every year, some 300,000 book manuscripts do not find a publisher, reports a publishing trade newsletter.

Certainly, writers have successfully carried out "Breaking Loose as a Full-Time Writer", as one article was titled. Jean Auel did. She was offered a promotion to an executive position in her firm. Instead, at age forty-something, she declined, resigned, and designed her Children of the Earth novels. But such success doesn't happen every day to everyday people. Those instances are only part of that bag of carrots dangled before us. It's irrational to believe that the act of "breaking loose" to "Give Yourself Time to Write" is sufficient warranty of success. Before chucking the check, one should first acquire a track record proving he truly can write to sell.

It also helps a lot to have another income, preferably with a medical plan, locked up before breaking out, whether the income be from a spouse willing and able to support a starting-outer, a retirement annuity, or a winning lottery ticket.

Once you quit your job, you need a full-time office away from home, advises another article. The reasons Why You Should Have Your Own Office: to command credibility; to provide a place to meet contact people; to assure yourself a quiet, uninterrupted place and space.

You don't really need a rebuttal, do you?

After your family sees you in print a couple of times, and especially after they see a couple of checks, you'll never again have to worry about credibility and what the article calls "gaining their respect". And before that time, they only view your writing as a "weirdo hobby", whether you have an office or not.

People don't come to writers. Writers go to people. Whoever heard of calling a college registrar with "For an article I'm preparing for Trendy Scholar, I'd like your enrollment figures for majors in microtechnological bacteriology. Please come to my office at 3:25 Thursday the 15th"? A large part of freelancing is footwork, and you can't do much of that from an office, anyway.

Okay, it's true: the typical home doesn't provide the world's most private place and space. If you're lucky enough to have a convertible room, it comes fairly close, sometimes. But commuting to an office, even to a one-person cubby-hole, isn't convenient for writers who, we already established, are "funny" anyway. In those middle-of-the-nights when words wanting to be written push away logs to be sawed, do you really want to dress and drive? When the family couch sprouts potatoes and you disappear to your desk or tabletop, isn't that a lot more acceptable to them and to your conscience than if you disappeared down the road? And, for the last nail, why would you want to divest yourself of a sum equal to two to four major sales a month just to own a rented office and another phone line?

I neither disparage any publication nor discourage any writer. Rather, I emphasize that professional writing, like any career requiring talent and skill, necessitates extended, extensive training and practice, becoming established, and a means to sustain life and family while doing it.

Be not deterred from dreaming, aspiring, creating. That's what you do and that's why you have to write. Just view whatever you read and hear from its proper rational perspective: Outrageous, illogical advice is meant to sell copies, not to sell you out.

SESSION 2

BEING IN TRAINING

SYMPOSIUM: PAYING YOUR DUES

Think of it as Schooling and Recreation

Fame, or Fortune?

Those "Other" Markets

A Byline is No Credit Line

Speaking of Humor

THINK OF IT AS SCHOOLING AND RECREATION

In July, 1984, I appeared in the doorway of Dr. Thomas Ferte's microscopic office at Western Oregon State College. I had attended Monmouth Institute on Creative Writing the previous summer; if the associate professor of English and founder of the Institute didn't recognize me, he didn't let on.

"I've retired from teaching. I'm ready to start writing."

Tom became grave and he dropped that grab-for-the-ring peptalk tone that writers use with writers. "You can expect it'll take about three years to get established," he counseled.

"Well, I don't have three years," I said in half-challenge, half-panic. "My golden jubilee isn't too far off, you know."

I joined Oregon Writers Colony and attended my first conference that October. I noticed then, and I've noticed many times since, the large proportion of writers and hopefuls who are 45, 50, retired and older. OWC member Mary Worthylake was past 60 when she wrote *Up in the Air* and hugging 70 when she published *School Bells Rang Everywhere.* Mickey Hickman was 74 when his first book was published; Sullivan had retired and Easterling was about to, and likewise for Joe Stein and Mabel Johnson and . . .

Now, when frazzled authors ask me, "When do I get time to write?" I answer cheerfully, "When the kids are grown or you retire or you have enough income to support your habit, which ever comes last." It's like telling the parents of pre-schoolers, with all honesty and sincerity, they really, truly will, some day 'way out there, grow up and leave home. It's not to discourage but to console.

The time factor is stunning. Crafters of fiction spend weeks on a short story, years on a novel. Writers of non-fiction spend hours and dollars to travel, interview, research, even before the first outline goes to the first editor.

My three years are up, and I guess I'm still not established, because the cost factor is still stunning, too. I still operate at a loss. I don't fool with mundanities like bottom lines, but Bob does; he knows how much, which year. Camera, car, conference; postage, professional dues and whatever else professionals do.

Here's a perspective.

Any skill requires training, practice; any profession requires schooling, training, practice, an internship. Consider the time spent "getting established" as a schooling period; your expenses, tuition; those returned manuscripts, homework; the tossed-out, the thrown away, the turned down as practice. You study to be a writer, just as surely as you would study to be a pharmacist; just as you'd practice to be a musician, a cake decorator, or a clerk-typist.

If you spend more than you earn on this year's writing, consider what you'd have spent if instead you had been golfing, flying, collecting antiques, or shopping under the flashing blue light.

After all, we write because we want to. It *is* our recreation.

Every time you contribute to your newsletter, or to your Arts News, or write a piece for the school or church program, you gain visibility. It's better than buying an ad because you're DEMONSTRATING what you can do.

FAME, OR FORTUNE?

As I placed the manila envelope on the outgoing mail heap, Bob asked, "Is this one for fame, or fortune?"

"They don't pay," I said.

On the other hand, Jeff Taylor of Corvallis, one of the four percenters, says firmly, "I never write for free anymore."

So why would anyone write for non-payment?

For publication credits. Everything you publish, byline, paying, or not, goes into your clip file. In your queries to paying markets, you state you've published two, ten or however many pieces. Editors want to know if you've published; they don't ask how much you've earned.

To see progress. Just as important, to show your family your progress. Seeing your work in print improves <u>their</u> attitude about what you're doing.

For barter. Helen Hecker, author of at least six books, writes a column-for free--for a national monthly. In return, the magazine carries an ad - for free - for her books. Authors, lecturers, and counselors write for New Age papers, neighborhood tabloids, arts news, religious periodicals, and the like; and in exchange, the papers plug their books and seminars.

For prestige. Prestige? For no pay? You bet. Some top - quality literary mags don't pay. Like *Black Ice*, like *Mississippi Mud*. Like *Calapooia Collage,* which in 1987 received 2000 submissions for its one-issue annual.

To create. Isn't all writing creative? Not at all. Sean Meyers, news editor of *Capital Press*, no less, dashes off poetry and short fiction for other editors; his agricultural weekly finds the editor's own stuff "does not meet our needs." For the same reasons, editors and staff writers of just about every publication large and small send pieces to other people's magazines.

To applaud someone else. Book reviews, articles for community arts papers, newsletters, trade, professional, local, regional print media. For whatever motive, there are times we <u>want</u> to recognize other people's accomplishments.

As a trial flight. "If you want to see if your book will fly, send a segment to a periodical," agent Michael Larson advised OWC members.

To pay dues in voluntary servitude for an organization which an individual wants to make go. Like contributing to a newsletter, writing a script for the church program, a sketch for the historical society's booklet. Like serving as an officer or on a committee for your writers' or publishers' organization.

To share information, to convey a message. Like this item you've just read, which first appeared as a donated piece in Oregon Writers Colony *Colonygram*.

Jeff Taylor, fulltime freelancer:

I'm happy to present no-fee workshops at libraries and at writers' meetings. Those contributions seldom fail to bring me editing and ghostwriting jobs.

Winifred Layton, editor, THE ARCHER:

My career was journalist and freelancer. Retired now, I edit THE ARCHER as a hobby. It keeps me in touch with poets, and with the literary world.

Dick Lutz, unpaid president, Northwest Association of Book Publishers:

As soon as I was nominated I started to get many tips and offers. The visibility that goes with the role is phenomenal.

> Of course there are markets for your writing. Editors have an incredible amount of space to fill and a crunchy deadline for filling it.
>
> TOM BANNAN

THOSE "OTHER" MARKETS

When you're looking for places to place your work, *Writer's Market* and, in the Northwest, *Writers Northwest Handbook* are the best places to start looking.

Fair warning though. Being listed doesn't tell all. A listing in a compendium doesn't always mean the publisher takes freelance work. Many daily newspapers apparently don't seek freelancers. They even ignore reviews and "press releases" that John Kremer urges authors and small presses to send in for publicity. Three dailies in northwest Washington state told me they do not take transom work from freelancers and according to several of my journalist acquaintances, the papers don't even have room for all the material their own staffs generate. The Northwest dailies, I found out the expensive way, don't even return return envelopes.

But a lot of periodicals would like to see you. Scout out those tabloids, especially the new, the small, the freebie, many of which are unlisted in writers' directories. Select one; write a few pieces or several proposals for short articles and send them in.

The community locals, those weeklies and neighborhood monthlies, appreciate and are likely to use material about fame and successes of hometown people. Do you know of a guy from Podunk who's achieved noteworthiness in The Big City? Send the Podunk Empire an article about the hometown fellow. With a photo; and be sure to identify him so the folks back in Podunk can see how the girl-swooner of 1972 grows chubby and bald.

Nor need you limit your submissions to small hometowns. Tom Bannan goes for the big-town Sunday supplements in faraway foreign lands, like California. An acquaintance of

Tom's is a pilot stationed in San Diego, but he also owns a vineyard in the Willamette Valley and the pilot's grapes have won several pieces of metal. He sent the story to the San Diego paper, and it flew.

There are other presses where you can break in, if you don't mind hustling. Search out those small community weeklies or monthlies. The North Town News, Community Times, so forth. Especially those with but a few ads, denoting austere budgets; they practically announce they're largely volunteer staffed, translate short-handed.

Look for Community Arts-type tabloids, likely to be found in libraries and music stores. Find the freebie special-focus publications distributed by New Age stores and counseling centers, by antique shops, farm suppliers, day care centers . . . get it?

If you can slant news, reviews, or a feature to the collegiate crowd, try the campus dailies or weeklies. Staffed principally by full-time students, those papers really appreciate transom copy. No pay, no byline, not for interlopers, at any rate-- remember, they are being turned out by students doing it for credit.

Try tapping colleges for another kind of writing job: for professors. Jeff Taylor edits, often ghosts entire pieces for university staffers. For $25 an hour. "When promoting or perishing depend on publishing, it's well worth it to them," Taylor says.

Local historical societies in the Northwest are voluminous publishers of books, booklets, quarterlies, tabloids, newsletters.

The reading room in your local library is a likely source for new, unheralded, unlisted, and small-circulation local publications.

Check out local and regional businesses, non-profit organizations, civic associations, fraternal organizations, senior centers, retirement villages, private schools, co-ops, granges, political, legislative, and lobby groups . . . Many of these produce newsletters, magazines, tabloids, pamphlets, booklets; and some of them even pay for material.

Challenge yourself to be the first on your writer's block to find new and different places for pieces.

ANOTHER ONE OF THOSE "HOW TO DEAL WITH REJECTIONS"

When I submitted an article after the editor's go-ahead, I promptly received it back with the "not right for us" form, exactly the same form magazines send when they reject the initial query. After some wound-nursing, I decided to "deal with rejection" constructively.

I boldly returned the manuscript to the editor who had signed the rejection, wondering why, since the initial query was accepted, the finished piece was not right for them. Then, I had the audacity to ask that editor for a critique. I also enclosed a check for $25, payable to her, noting that I'd seen numerous ads for manuscript critiques at about that price.

The article: "New Insights to Memory: Implications for New Strategies." The magazine: *Learning,* a professional publication for elementary and middle school teachers. The informational content I had collated from several very recent pieces and from research abstracts; the applications came from teachers I know and from my own experience. It contained sidebars, lists, specifics. I thought it one of my best pieces.

It came as a mild surprise when the editor answered. At first the comments wounded me a new; but from them I've gained valuable lessons. (In fact, the process bears out one of the strategies in the article: "Traumatize them into learning.")

Critique: "The title promised something new. There wasn't. The topic, since it's important to teachers, has already been addressed in *Learning.*" Lesson: If it's something you've read a lot about, it's past marketability. Lesson, also: Assume a topic of professional import will be treated in professional publications as soon as the news is new.

Critique: "You used other people's quotes and anecdotes. Be direct - just say what you want said." Lesson: Each publication has its own style; magazines do not like to be eclectic. *Northwest Women in Business* wants quotes and anecdotes; *Learning* does not. Writers need to study--not just read, but study - the magazines they write for.

Critique: "I had a problem with your organization." When writing it, I had grappled for days with the article's organization and sequence, and despite the criticism, I still (stubbornly?) thought it well-done. If there's a lesson here, it's that personal preferences do influence an editor's decision.

Only that once was I brassy enough to question a rejection; chances are that only that one editor would have responded so graciously. I'm glad it happened. She also returned my check. She said she was just doing her job.

Attorney Leonard duBoff, author of *The Law (In Plain English) For Writers*, advises us to save rejection slips. To IRS, they're evidence of professional intent. Hint: Date them as you receive them; file together by calendar year.

> After an IRS rep presented tax facts to NABP, members just shook their heads in confusion. It's easier just to pay your 28%, they agreed. With the complicated new simplified rules, you could pay an accountant $100 to find $25 in tax savings.

A BYLINE IS NO CREDIT LINE

I checked myself into our local hospital for one of those X- Rays that's a good idea for women who are, um, mature. The first half hour of my "visit" (why does the medical profession like to make it sound like a social call?) was spent establishing that someone would probably pay. I'd gone through the routine before, when I took my mother-in-law in the time she was having her cardiac arrest. If you die before they admit you, do they charge?

The smiling lady poised pen above blank form.

"Occupation?"

"Writer."

Smile dropped; pen remained raised.

"Anything else?"

"Retired teacher."

"Anything else?"

"I help around the farm."

The unsmiling lady wrote: "Housewife."

We were not amused.

Then, hoping for better prospects, the admissions clerk resumed smiling and asked, "Husband's occupation?"

"Retired teacher."

Sigh. "Anything else?"

"Farmer."

The lady printed, "Retired."

Back at the ranch, I told Bob, "I guess retired is a better credit line than teacher or farmer. And being a writer is the least credit of all."

KAREN KARBO, Screenwriter:

Creators of comedy are serious --
it's serious work.
If people who try to write comedy
don't have a funny view of the world,
it won't be comedy.

SPEAKING OF HUMOR

Elizabeth Pomoda, literary agent,
San Francisco:

Humor is a very personal thing. What one reader enjoys might not work at all for another. Yours doesn't work for me.

Joyce de Monnin, Senior Writer,
Northwest Women in Business:

Humor is very personal. It's based on truth, truth with a twist but not twisted; not raucous but subtle.

John Kremer, Author,
Ad-Lib Publications:

I find it distracting when one shifts from humor to seriousness. I wonder how they mean it, and the seriously intended content loses its credibility.

Tom Ferte
Teacher:

It's hard to maintain humor for more than a couple of pages.

Paul Pearsall in Superimmunity, Master Your
Emotions and Improve Your Health:

There's no question that laughter is good for you. The presence of humor is one of the strongest predictors of the absence of mental illness.

"Demand for humor is cyclic. Right now it's down," agent Elizabeth Pomada wrote in 1986. (Well, actually, it was a rejection.)

At the very same time, librarians at one large and two smallishes stated that humor is in high demand, there aren't enough funny books to go around, and their most-requested author is Art Buchwald.

Carla Emery, novelist, editor, journalist:
Don't let humor try to pass for substance.

Ritch Davidson, Senior Vice Emperor, Playfair, Inc:
T-Cell production, which is essential for the body's immune system, is increased during laughter.

In the 1987-88 season, most programs in the Neilson Top 20 are comedies. People want more to be entertained, to lighten up after a day's work followed by the news.
Gannet columnist, Jan. 1988

Humor has ascended to scholarly echelons. A new quarterly (debut spring, 88), HUMOR: INTERNATIONAL JOURNAL OF HUMOR RESEARCH publishes papers and research reports in strict academic style and format. As writers of humor know, writing humor is serious business.

"People in agriculture develop a humorous outlook because it's a tough business," writes Ann Frey Cummins. Farmers are laughing so hard at her CATTLE ANNIE it's 1988's best seller around the auction barns.

By the way, you as a writer ought to study CATTLE ANNIE for its innovative, out-of-the-ordinary punctuations. At last, the printed page captures the inflections of real talkin'.

SESSION 3

BEING SPECIFIC

Queries: Letter of Sale

Sample Query Letters

Article Proposals

Sample Proposals

First-Person Resources

Sources of Resources

Kiddie - Liter-ers

How to be Trendy

Scriptwriting

GAIL TYCER:

If you can write and write well, you're going to be a wanted commodity.

QUERIES:
LETTERS OF SALE

Writing is the craft of producing a polished, professional piece.

Selling is the result of composing a skillful query.

A query is your letter to the editor of the publication you intend to sell to. A query is a question: "Would you like to see the piece?" Or, "May I submit the article on spec?" But it isn't mandatory to include a sentence punctuated with a question mark: "I'd like to send the article, on spec, for your review" is still a query.

Don't underestimate your query's importance. "A well written query lets me know if a writer can write," says Pat Vargas, editor of *Gurney's Gardening News*. "I suggest they give some time to making that query sparkle." She adds, "I get a lot of these: 'Are you interested in an article on tomatoes?' My answer is always NO."

Because the query is the editor's introduction to the writer, the letter must be well-written--a sample of the writer's craftsmanship, as professional as the submitted work will be.

If your query is a good one, you're likely to catch the editor's favorable eye, even if you've never yet been published. The reason? Believe this, editors told us they just don't see a lot of great ones.

"It is a rare query letter than conforms to all the basics of submission," writes Chuck Jonak of *Kiwanis* magazine.

Wee Wisdom often receives submissions which violate the level- one basics, says Verle Bell; and so does *Ruralite*.

Adele Malott of *Friendly Exchange* speaks of "one heckuva query--skillfully written and targeted to my audience."

So just what is a heckuva query, and exactly what are the basics?

THE BASICS

First, form and format.

It's a business letter, single spaced, typed on good-quality bond paper with clear black ribbon. Editors get originals, not copies.

Second and foremost, it's a sales pitch. You're selling yourself as a writer, selling the writing you write.

Here are your selling points.

1. **Article Opener.** Editors like to see your beginning paragraph. "A writer can make points by including the lead of his proposed article," says Pat Vargas.

2. **Content and focus.** Briefly explain what the article's about, and the slant or viewpoint that makes it appropriate for the particular publication. The editor wants to know how it's "targeted to my audience", remember?

Your summary might be better said in article-style rather than in I, II , A - B - C outline form. Adele Malott writes, "I do not think the formal outline . . . shows off the writer's writing skills, which I want to see."

3. **Sources**. From whom, where, and/or what sources come information, anecdotes.

4. **Approximate length**. *Writer's Market*, as well as the guides most publications furnish on request, state the usual article length the publication wants. You can tell the editor your anticipated word count with "The article will be approximately 900 words (or whatever they specify)." If you don't you can say, "Please advise concerning your preferred article length." Or, " . . . 1200 words, or according to your specifications."

Include a sentence stating the availability of photos, drawings, graphs, sidebars, if you'll be able to provide them.

5. **Your qualifications**. If your professional training is applicable to the topic, say so. If you've been published before, say that, too--not a bibliography, but a statement such as "My writing credentials include four published articles in regional periodicals." You can name the publications if you wish, if it will serve a positive purpose. If you've had printed a letter to the editor in Podunk Weekly, it won't impress the editor of Slick Times; neither is it in your best interests to tell the editor of *Presbyterian Survey* you've sold to *Athiest Review*.

Present yourself as positively and professionally as you can. He who tooteth not his own horn, the same shall not be tootethed. You're a salesindividual, remember.

It's a good idea to mention you'll "submit on spec" (you're speculating). You're saying you understand that a go-ahead from the editor is not his commitment to buy, that you know the editor wants to look first. In responding, the editor will tell you to submit on spec, anyway, but your saying so first speaks for your professionalism. It shows you understand the process.

And, oh, yes -- Editors like for you to accomplish all the above in one page, or, at most, a page and a half.

PAST TENSE?

Should you compose a query in past tense, as though you've already done the work; or in future tense, as going to write?

Both.

Imply you've already done some research and now you'll write the piece specifically for them, according to their instructions.

First, you've had to do some finding out before you know there's something to be said. At the outset, your query makes a factual statement about the topic.

Interview, ask, gather data, get quotes and comments, and then use a few in your query. Then, in your letter, say something like, "Resource persons are . . . "; "I've interviewed . . . " (past tense). That way, an editor knows you actually have a basis of information -- and a story.

Editors, most of them freelancers themselves, also know that writers will actually extract useful information from only about half their prospective resources persons--and that's an optimistic fraction. Therefore, if you say, "My resources will include . . . ", or, "I plan to interview . . . " (future tense), the editor knows from experience you may not, in fact, procure any quotes and comments at all.

Secondly, tense your verbs to show that you will write the article specifically for that publication. You certainly don't want to leave even a hint that you're hoping to just route along a piece already written and rejected by someone else.

CLIPS

As *Writer's Market* notes, skillions of publications want to see what you've already published: "Query with clips." Perhaps, from those magazines, the real message is that they aren't too interested in newcomers.

So what if you have no clips?

Easy. Choose publications that don't ask for them. Many don't.

Many editors aren't impressed by clips and don't read them. Naomi Woolever of *National Grit* says, "The manuscript will tell us what we need to know about the author's skills as a writer." *Ruralite* agrees: "So long as the story is worthwhile, clips are irrelevant."

Other clip comments: "A previously published piece might not show how well a writer writes but how well an editor has edited."

"I have no way of knowing how much an editor has overhauled a piece. I don't read clips."

Pat Jossey, former editor of *Earthtone* magazine, told Oregon Writers Colony members "Good photos sell stories. If it's a tossup between manuscripts, I'll take the one with artwork. I even take the one with good photos sometimes when the manuscripts aren't otherwise a tossup."

> MIKE LOWERY, FOCAL POINT PHOTOGRAPHY, DALLAS, OR:
>
> For black and white prints, most journalists and photographers use 400 speed film.
> It's versatile with a good grain.
> For color slides, Ektachrome 200 is the most popular.
> It's a versatile all-purpose speed, good color, decent grain, and will transfer to useable black and white prints.
> If the film name ends in color, it's for prints; chrome is for slides.

If you'll provide photos, say so in your query. If you don't know what kind, ask, "Do you prefer black and white glossies, negatives, transparencies, or contact sheets?"

Today's cameras do more; you guess less. Get yourself a good 35 mm camera (Not expensive. Good.) and learn to use it. Many camera shops (Not discount stores. Photography shops, manned by photographers.) offer a free photo course with camera purchase. Buying from a pro gives you more dollars worth of expertise now and service later than you'll save by buying discount. Discount cameras are usually sold by salesmen, not by photographers.

SAMPLE QUERIES

"How to Write a Query" articles are easy to find. But finding actual queries in print is not.

The "sample query" samples we've found are seldom actual queries; they're instructions written in query format. One of the best is in *Writers Northwest Handbook,* 2nd Edition, pp 34, 35. Sample queries which are actually queries are in 1988 *Writer's Market.*

When we asked 23 editors across the country for copies of exemplary queries, every one of them declined.

"We haven't the rights to queries and can't release them."

"If I sent a sample, too many authors would copy its style, and we wouldn't be seeing individual creativity."

In the absence of others, then, we furnish some of ours. For whatever reason, they worked. But remember, please, our words of Welcome: We do not write gospels; there are no absolutes.

A word, first, about format. When your query begins with your proposed lead, do you double-space the lead? Opinions of freelancers differ; I'm inclined to think it's a matter of your own preference. On the one hand, a double-spaced lead does establish that it is the lead; on the other hand, it's almost impossible to compose a one-page query if it's double-spaced. As Martha Kay Renfrow says, "Be yourself."

SAMPLE QUERY LETTER

My Address

Their Address

Dear Editor:

> The daughter of a Michigan couple speaks of finding her parents a place without a yard to keep up. A Florida widow moves to a condominium. A Washington state man, only 57, worries he'll soon have to give up his yard.
>
> "Nonsense!" exclaims a 73-year-old Oregonian whose back yard, she boasts, "is like a park." Charles Laird, 76, agrees. "If you took me out of my yard, you'd soon put me in a box." Like gardeners across the land, Laird has devised means to lighten the labor and continue to enjoy the shade of his own tree.

I'd like to present GURNEY'S GARDENING NEWS readers with labor-saving shortcuts to a nice yard and garden in "Gardening: Lightening the Labor."

Slant: Nearly everyone loves his yard and garden. In fact, while interviewing for this article I discovered that grandchildren is only the <u>second</u> favorite topic of most people. Yet while we basically enjoy the work and take pride in the results, the time comes when most of us have to cut back on the amount or the intensity of the labor. Whether it be encroachments of career or other commitments upon our time, or the fact of slowing down as we grow older, many readers--especially women living alone--welcome specific, concrete means of lightening the labor.

Development: Several Western gardeners reveal strategies they have developed for lightening the labor of yard work. A majority of people interviewed are retirees, some with physical disabilities, including a 60-year-old who has been in a wheelchair for over a decade but who still works with her flowers.

A chiropractic physician advises readers how to prevent pain, and how to care for pains and strains when they occur.

Sidebar: Do's and don'ts for lifting, bending, and handling tools, depicted in black and white photos. Releases included.

Article length: Please specify.

The article will be delivered to you within three weeks of your go-ahead.

Sincerely,

Name and signature

The editor's response included instructions on length, photos, and a date by which the submission was to be received, along with the phrase "on spec."

This query was early in my writing efforts, when I didn't know about mentioning prior publications (very few at this point, and fewer were paid). It didn't seem to matter to GURNEY'S.

SAMPLE QUERY LETTER

My address

Their Address

Dear Editor:

> "In all the stores, Christmas things are out, right next to the Halloween masks. They're really pushing the season."
>
> "Hmpf. There should be no Christmas merchandise displayed until after Thanksgiving."
>
> Those sentiments are expressed every year, but only by our city cousins. Long-termers in the bush country of Alaska, the Yukon, the Northwest Territory, and even in the Okanogan and the outback of Idaho, know that if they wait until Halloween to think about Christmas, it's already too late.

"Christmas at Halloween? It's Already Too Late" will explain to NORTHWEST LIVING readers who don't already understand why folks living in the remote spots of the Northwest have to get with Christmas even before they pass around the Halloween candy. The article, approximately 800 words, enumerates the reasons rural residents need to commence the season so early. How early? According to the timetable in the article, in August: "Search for address book. Check with family matriarch for updated addresses."

The piece is most suited for September or October. It will be illustrated with color transparencies of December in rural Alaska, and a store display of Halloween, Christmas, and Valentine merchandise, all together, in a village store. Valentine? Oh, yes, that represents the date bush dwellers can expect to receive their Christmas packages if they fail to prepare before Halloween. I know. The first year (of 20) we were in Alaska, we actually did receive our Christmas package--from grandparents who refused to think Christmas until after Thanksgiving--on February 14.

Signature

SAMPLE QUERY LETTER

Address

Address

Dear Editor:

In a six-mile stretch along the Van Duzer Corridor are fifteen arts and crafts shops, all featuring the works of local artisans. For some, those who are fulltime businesspersons, professionals, and workingpeople, art is an avocation, an expression; for others, their art itself is their life. And in this mountain-and-woodland setting at the crest of the Coast Range, nature nurtures a kind of Bohemian existence, an inducement, perhaps, to draw out the moods and creativity inherent in the artistic.

Joe Huff of Pedee claims there are, within a 20-mile radius of the Coast Range, more professional-quality artists than in any other portion of the country. And John Stein of Renton thinks he knows why. On an early autumn tour of the Polk-Lincoln County mountains, he proclaimed, "It's a place where people can get everything together in an earthy perspective. It's the kind of place that frees one to create."

For your magazine I'd like to write an article about the artists who live near the Corridor, focusing upon their perceptions of this setting as an influence on their work. Specific painters and craftspersons will be profiled.

"Artists of Van Duzer Corridor", approximately 1200 words, with captioned photos for your selection, would fit a 4-column spread. Photos can be either transparencies or B/W prints or contacts, as you specify. I have published both, although black and white is my better medium.

Sig
Name

The editor's response: "Please call -- we need to discuss." I did and we did. She liked the concept of the article, but Van Duzer Corridor isn't close enough to their region. I went instead to Seal Rock, talked to people, lost myself in the Oregon Coast muse, and got a far better piece than I'd have from the original area proposed.

This was a case of an editor liking a concept, but needing to refine for a different geographical focus. It was one of my best pieces, for one of the best magazines.

For what it's worth if anything, I notice that on none of these queries did I mention any particular qualifications or prior publication credits.

ARTICLE PROPOSALS

> SUSAN STANLEY:
>
> Send several article proposals together to show an editor you're an idea person, that you'd be a steady, reliable contributor, able to supply regular copy.

> TOM BANNAN:
>
> A proposal can be briefer, sketchier than a query. It describes content and sources of information, perhaps without as acute a focus, and doesn't necessitate a snappy opener. I prefer proposals.

Proposal--query. Is there a difference? When is one better than the other?

Writer's Market glossary does not list "proposal" at all and defines "query" very simply: "A letter to an editor aimed to get his interest in an article you want to write." In that case, query and proposal are the same, and writers and instructors appear to use the terms interchangably. Other writers, however, distinguish Because words convey precise shades of meaning, let's differentiate:

Proposal: (1) shorter, less detailed than a query;
(2) multiple proposals may be submitted together;
(3) may be less formal;
(4) therefore appropriate principally for editors one knows or has worked with.

When Tom Bannan introduced the proposal to his class at Chemeketa Community College, he illustrated with samples that were in length and substance essentially the same as a query. His proposals were in query-letter format; one included the article's lead paragraph and one did not. They were not sharply different from queries.

Directly below the salutation, Tom types in capital letters:

THIS IS AN ARTICLE PROPOSAL.

On the other hand, the proposals Susan Stanley showed her group sessions at a Willamette Writers conference were very short, a paragraph each, several to a typed page, with a cover letter for all. Once, she explained, she submitted to a large weekly publication a batch of 25 article ideas - not detailed, but topic and focus only. "I hoped she (the editor) would accept half of them. She took twenty-one," Stanley said.

She hastened to add that submitting sketchy ideas an armload at a time is a strategy suitable only for an editor who already knows that writer and her work, and when the editor knows the writer is thoroughly familiar with the publication. "Nobody would assign 21 articles at a time unless he knew the writer could and would produce," she cautioned.

A Salem freelancer sent a batch of three article proposals to *Stepping Out*. "I wanted to demonstrate that I understood their content and focus, that I had many ideas and resources, and that I could provide copy on a regular basis," she said. Each proposal was three paragraphs, each was on a separate page, and a cover letter introduced the writer and stated credits and credentials.

The editor didn't take any of the proposals, but told the writer she would be considered when assignments were next made. "It didn't matter much that those specific ideas weren't what the editor wanted," the author explained. "It did matter that I'm now known to her."

Bannan, Stanley, and others suggest this protocol for proposal submissions:

(a) If the proposal is the only one being submitted, use regular query letter format, business letter form.

(b) If multiples are being sent together, use a cover letter and type one proposal per page if they are three or more paragraphs.

(c) If several very short ones are being sent together, you can run them together, triple-spaced between items. "This approach is appropriate only if you're a regular contributor. Brevity and informailty won't do unless you're in long standing good standing," warns Andi Zylscha. "I give the boss just a line or two of proposal; but then I churn stuff out all the time, several pieces per issue." Zylscha writes for a monthly tabloid.

Following are illustrative samples of article proposals.

SAMPLE ARTICLE PROPOSALS

<u>ARTICLE PROPOSAL</u>

Topic: Home Schooling

Focus: State - to - local--adaptable and expandable

The U.S. Department of Education estimates that 260,000 American children are now receiving their schooling at home; as of December 1 our state reported 2600 home study students. Both the state and the local school districts impose specific regulations for study at home, including attendance, curriculum, and standardized testing. In our state, 23% of home-study pupils scored in the upper 23 percentile on those tests--that's the 77th percentile or above.

This regional article will include: statistics for our state--number of students, teachers, test scores; state and local regulations. From parents who teach their own kids, reasons for choosing home schooling; advantages and disadvantages. From school personnel in local district, comments as to how home school transfers do in comparison with their peers.

Although this is short, I'd put it on a separate page. The space at the bottom gives an editor room to write comments, particular instructions.

ARTICLE PROPOSAL

Topic: A self-supporting community theatre

Focus: State (or regional, or local, or the arts, or . . . adapt to specific publication)

According to its manager, Salem's Pentacle Theatre is the only self-supporting community theatre in Oregon. The paradox, according to performing arts critics in Dallas, Salem, Newport, and Eugene, is that Salem is one of the state's communities least supportive of the arts.

Not only is Pentacle fiscally successful, it's busy: a show on stage and one in rehearsal just about all the time. Actors, directors, technicians, musicians--all volunteers, they swarm to Pentacle in limitless supply, some from a hundred miles away. What's the theatre's attraction? How is it so successful?

The article will include a profile of its manager, a director, and photos. A 1200-word piece with four or five photos will fit a two-page layout.

The following may be submitted together on a single page.

ARTICLE PROPOSALS

Title: 14 Ways Parents Can Help Their Kids in School

Parents and teachers present practical, pragmatic, easy, uncomplicated ways that parents can help their youngsters do well in school. Ideas from parents and educators from Alaska, Minnesota, North Carolina, Maine, California, and Washington.

Title: How to Interperet Those Exuberant Form Letters Superfamilies Send at Christmas

When we receive those formletters-in-lieu of Christmas cards, most of us who have normal, average families (rowdy kids and a couple of setbacks every year) simply feel bad about ourselves. This sample of a glowing, superachievement Christmas letter contains an interperetation to make you feel better: it shows how the phrases are turned so that families who write up that glib blitter are really doing no better than yours.

Title: Ralph Carlton's Twenty Thousand Mile Bicycle

Ralph Carlton's bike recently logged its twenty thousandth mile. A plain two-wheeled, muscle-powered bicycle. He'll tell where it's been, and reveal the bike's formula for a long, active life. And the piece will convey Carlton's personality. The long-time Central Point resident is 69.

Three Approaches to Marketing:

One is to write what you want to say and then shop for a publication that wants to hear it. This is most often done in fiction, poetry, book manuscripts.

A second is to shop for a publication and then tailor something for it specifically. "Hmmm, here's Grain Grower's Quarterly. I think I'll write something for them." You write what they want to see.

The third is a combination. Begin with your own idea, find a publication your subject fits, then develop your idea according to their slant. This is the way most freelance marketing is accomplished.

FIRST PERSON RESOURCES

The writer of a freelance article is not the expert on the subject. A writer is collator, analyst, spokesperson. And even if the freelancer is an expert, his own information, to be credible to editor and reader, needs to be supported. The difference between op-ed - a zilchy market - and an informative piece - a bottomless basket - is the citation of multiple resources.

Your wildflower variety of writer searches periodical indexes, abstracts, newspaper clip files, seeking out what's been said, what's known. He gleans information that was undoubtedly accurate when it was published. But the lag between writing and publishing may be a year, often more. And if the wildflower's sources also searched the files for previously published sources . . .

The cultivated writer, in contrast, goes directly to the experts, tapping new, updated, unrecycled, never-before-quoted views and experiences.

"Yeah but. I don't know any experts. And I couldn't get to them if I did."

You don't have to know anyone. You only have to know how to find out who's there, and where. After that, the only place you have to go is your office -- or kitchen table, or desk in the bedroom, or whatever constitutes your office.

REACH OUT AND PUT THE TOUCH ON SOMEONE

When your work is in its formulative stage, your most valuable tool is telephone, not typewriter. It's your best means of making contact -- and getting response.

Can't afford to write by phone? Compute:

For each letter you write . . .

A. Compose, edit, produce finished copy: one hour for first letter; plus type/copy time for each subsequent one.

B. For each piece of correspondence: 44 cents for postage, approximately 7 cents for two envelopes, letterhead.

C. Turn-around time for responses: 3 to 4 weeks.

D. Rate of response for written requests for info: staggeringly low - one in five is generous. To compensate, you must plan to send 10 inquires to have two or three sources for your article.

Despite the exasperations of answering machines, being put on hold, and information desks that don't know any information, I keep my hand: Telephoning is the best practical option.

Before you call, you'll of course prepare a snappy spiel. Who, where, what you are, why you're calling.

Don't exaggerate. DO NOT say "I'm with National Scoop Tabloid" when in fact you're merely considering querying Nat Scoop. Tell them you're a freelancer preparing an article about the socioeconomic effects of the new scoop technology. Lots of experts have tried freelancing, too, and they will understand.

Then, ask some specific questions. Once they have a handle on your scoop, they'll run from there, augmenting with additional comments and quotes you can use.

You already know your phone call is likely to be answered by a machine, a secretary who doesn't know, or a four-year-old. Be undaunted. Introduce yourself, state your purpose, and tell him, her, or it what time you'll call back, leave your area code and number. Sometimes the party will return your call, but most often they'll wait for you to spend your nickel. Do it.

WRITTEN INQUIRIES: SAMPLER

At times a letter is appropriate. Following is a letter requesting professional comment for an article. The letter was sent to four professionals.

SAMPLE LETTER TO RESOURCE PERSON

Your Return Address
Include phone number

1 Name, Title
Inside Address

Greeting:

2 I am a freelance writer preparing articles about quality time with children. I would like you to contribute your expertise, as offered in Purdue Contacts. Any comment you offer will be credited with each use. You will be sent a copy of all published pieces in which your name appears.

My articles will define "quality time" and put into pragmatic everyday, ongoing interaction between parent and child. It will enumerate the many means by which quality time can be achieved.

3 A network news report stated working mothers spend, on average, 11 minutes of quality time per day with their child, while the "full-time" mom spends 13 minutes. The biggest surprise is that mothers of all work arrangements spend so little. Why so little? Perhaps it's the definition. Quality time, explained the reporter, is time spent in educational activities. While nearly any stimulus and perception can be educational, the reporter clearly meant "instructional" time. So is the time spent brushing a child's hair not quality? Nor having kids go along for shopping, helping with yard work, wrapping gifts, nor listening to their stories in the car and at the table?

4 How do you, yourself, define "quality time"? What are some quality interactions with kids? And how about the parental attitudes of interaction: are they not significant to quality also? Supervising homework, for example, is negative if parent berates and criticizes.

5 I shall appreciate a few comments, a few viewpoints. SASE is enclosed for your response. Thank you for participating.

Signature
Name

LETTER TO RESOURCE PERSON...Notes and explanantion

1 Business letter format

2 Present yourself immediately: who, why, what you're asking. This is no time for "grabby openers." Tell your contact where, how you heard of him; assure him he'll receive credit and see his name in print if it gets there.

3 Explain your view, what you plan to do with it, where you're coming from and where the piece is going. The contact can then speak to your specific focus.

4 Present specific leading questions. People will take it from there, probably adding their own.

5 Be brief, a page if possible...Note SASE. Contact knows you're serious, not just curious.

There's a story...isn't there always, or why would we write?

I sent this letter to a professor listed in Purdue Contacts, *a media resource blessed by the University. After five silent weeks I called Contacts editor, who put me in touch with the prof. He said he didn't know what I wanted or why.*

The prof explained in long phrases he doesn't believe in qualtiy time, that it's a nonentity hyped up by the pop psych media. Of my SASE, he said, "I don't have it." Translate pitched out. But he offered to "engage in a dialogue at a later date, not by letter but by telephone, where I can explain my position."

Sometimes you determine a resource is not a useful one.

I sent four such letters and received two answers. Then I phoned three other professionals in the field and got material for the article.

Letters don't always work even when you follow the protocols.

TRUZZWORDS

The word was new and fresh. It caught on. Trendy. It became jargonized. A buzzword. It grew stale, its meaning mutated to fuzz.

A truzzword.

Truzzwords, through overuse are uncreative; by misuse, imprecise, full of sound and meaning nothing. Conversational trendtalk with peers is one thing; truzzwriting is something else: pflupfth.

Today's rankletruzzes:

SPECIAL. Formerly, superlative quality; or a weekend sale. Now a term of religious favor, as best intoned by Church Lady; or mentally impaired. "God made my goat just spe-eesshh-ull." Naturally my last birthday card was "To a special Mom."

STATE-OF-THE-ART. The arts are performing, fine, and literary; states are excitement, Michigan, and being. States are not automotive dashboards and intelligent can openers. It's the <u>cats</u> that are intelligent, when they <u>hear</u> the can opener.

GREAT. Originally indicated size or fame, now a passing tone in supermarket ads. "Great for snacks . . ."; "Great for menus." Great menus are the printed ones in the state-of-the-art restaurants writers can't afford, not the prices-slashed in-store specials.

CLEARLY. "Clearly, our mission is . . ." It's politicalprose, and the clear part is that we can see right through it.

Replace truzzes with your own creations. Punnery is fun. "We have cowslips in our pasture." No, not flowers. Slippery spots I slip on. *Cowslips* is a nice euphemistic replacement for that scowldrawing beepword.

Wimp. From its very sound, you can tell what it means. It's a descriptive sound, so overworked it's run out of hemoglobin. So why not play with your own sounds. "He's a quink." Or its opposite: "He's a boomarex." Or "School lunch is vomarf." And "My fluffluv cat."

Brightscribe with sparklephrase.

SOURCES OF RESOURCES

It isn't difficult to find knowledgeable individuals eager to answer your questions. Most professionals like their names in credit lines as well as you like yours in bylines. Publication gives them as much or more professional boost as it does you.

You don't need celebrities. A Ph.D at your local community college is just as informed and opinionated as one at Bigstate U. The nutrition counselor at Your Town Eating Disorders Clinic holds the same Master's degree as the director of Well Known Program Center in Megopolis County; your own pastor's words are as inspiring as Peale's. And, anyway, Peale doesn't answer his mail.

In fact, few celebrities answer their mail, not, at least, letters from ordinary people. So don't bother to spend your currency or plastic for a "celebrity address book."

Utilize experts who live in the geographical area of your intended publication. If you intend to submit to *Metro Month* contact sourcepersons who work in Metro's circulation area. You still can "spoke" the article to subsequent markets. If, for example, you plan to submit essentially the same piece to *Wide West and Interprairie Papers*, add to your resources someone from Nevada, Arizona, and Nebraska.

Telephone Books. Libraries carry phone books of many towns and cities over America and Canada. Use yellow page listings.

College Catalogs list faculty names and departments. Consider especially the smaller schools - their faculty seem more accessible and they appreciate the professional recognition. "Better than writing the article myself," said a Linfield College professor.

Directories of Organizations list organizations, their purpose, address, name of contact, phone number. Many are 800 numbers. Organizations are often in the business of providing information; they are your most willing sources. Directories are in libraries.

800 Telephone Directory. In libraries.

Congressinal Staff Directory. Name, address, phone number of each member of Congress; staff names, titles. Committees and members; executive departments and personnel, independent agencies; Senate and House state delegations. Key word subject index. In libraries.

Encyclopedia of Associations. Name, address, contact and/or administrator; phone number. Purpose and functions of each association.

College Resource Directories are published by many schools. To be included, faculty is expected to pledge himself available to the media including journalists and writers. (Individuals don't always keep the commitment, as has been mentioned.)

Directory of Experts, Authorities, & Spokespersons: "The Talk Show Guest Directory" Mitchell P. Davis, Ed. Broadcast Interview Source, 2500 Wisconsin Ave. N.W., Washington D.C. 20077-3240. $25.00.

3,569 sources indexed by 5,378 topics. Listings by both topic and individual/organization.

Individuals listed in this book have ASKED to be there; the publisher includes reporting forms so users can keep Davis advised as to effectiveness of persons listed.

If you get only one book for finding people, this one is the one.

To find out how to find out, your best overall resources person is your librarian.

For current information and statistics on the local and regional scene, ask the people at your County Extension Service, Children and Family Services, Mental Health Division, or office of the County Clerk. Those agencies seem to have all the information there is or they know where to get it, and they're willing to talk to you.

I never have trouble getting interviews for freelance pieces. Everyone likes their name in print.

If I were to get another degree it would be in psych. Almost any freelance piece is enhanced with a quote from a psyschologist.

You could conduct business by phone for a week and never talk to a person. I think pretty soon my machine talks to your machine.

MICKEY BELLMAN:
Valuable sources of up-to-date facts and figures are Department of Interior, Bureau of Land Management, Department of Agriculture, and various state and Federal agencies.
In most population centers, these resources are only a short-distance call away.

I'd rather talk to your machine than have to hold for hours listening to your elevator tunes.

KIDDIE LIT-ERS

In what category is the highest-quality overall writing?

It's juveniles, says Winifred Morris, who's published by Atheneum. Why? Because the principal buyers of kids' literature are librarians and teachers, and they insist on exemplary stuff.

Here's encouragement for Northwesterners: Portland and vicinity "is becoming known as fertile ground for children's writing by Eastern publishers," says Ellen Howard, regional advisor for Society of Children's Bookwriters. Susan Hirschman, editor of Greenwillow Books (juvenile imprint of William Morrow) told *Alaska Native Magazine* that her firm is particularly impressed by the high quality of children's books coming from Alaskan authors.

Children's books and magazines are steady markets, and growing. But writing for kids is Hard! . . . To! . . . Do!

From an old hand who's taught reading to kids of every single grade level, here are some hints and how's.

Define your readers both by age and reading level. They aren't the same. That's why it's tough.

First, fewer than half of fourth graders read at fourth grade reading level, for example. Secondly, grade-level *instructional* reading level - material in textbooks and presented with guided instruction--is not the same as *recreational* reading level. Material kids select for independent reading for pleasure is generally one to two steps below their instructional level.

In the third place, youngsters generally prefer reading about protagonists older than themselves. So if you intend for that fourth grader to to take your book to her favorite spot under a cool shadetree, or to curl around the kitten in a soft over-stuffed corner, or any of the other wonderful quiet private places where youngsters experience literature, then you need to write about topics that are two or three years older, and at a reading level a step and a half down.

There exists a dire need for well-written stories of "high interest - low vocabulary." Teen and young adult subjects written at third, fourth grade reading level. Without being patronizing, condescending, or down-looking. *Scholastics* Publications specializes in this kind of literature, and from this old campaign-ribboned veteran's viewpoint, they do a wonderful job.

Grade level determination isn't just vocabulary, either. Readability is also determined by sentence length and complexity; by placement of subject, verb, introductory clauses, modifiers, and adjective and adverbial phrases; by number of syllables in a sentence; by types and frequency of punctuations; and by the literary subtleties corresponding to intellectual age: inference, characterizations, generalizations, and the content of the story line itself.

Two ways to check your own composition for juvenile readers.

First, study quality material. It's in your library. Assess literature of various age, reading, and interest levels. Evaluate for form, content, structure, style. Let those be your gauge for your own composition.

Secondly, give your own writing a readability assessment. Several easy-to-use instruments are available. Janet Mann of Linn-Benton Education Service District, Albany, Oregon, says the most frequently used tools are Fry Readability Scale, Dale-Chall Formula, the Spache, Flesch, Raygor, and Gunning-Fog formulas. At least one of those assessments is most likely available at any elementary school.

In the $40 range, a software readability formula called *Apple: Finding Readability* is available from Sunburst Communications, Room G-7, 39 Washington Avenue, Pleasantville, NY 10570, phone 1-800-431-1934. When a paragraph is entered in the computer, the program analyzes for factors cited above, then determines the passage's reading level. Similar programs are now or soon shall be available. No serious children's writer should forego one.

Children's literature is among the decade's finest writing, and kiddie lit enjoys a growing market. It's a brighter prognosis than ever for children's authors; but kiddie lit - ers need to heed what kids can read.

EILEEN WEEKS, Salem, children's author:

I cannot rave enough about the course in writing for children offered by the Institute of Children's Literature, West Redding, Connecticut 06876-0701. Phone 1-800-243-9645.

The program provides individualized, one-on-one instruction by correspondence. Each piece is evaluated, critiqued, and, yes, marked up like crazy, and returned in a timely manner. Their staff includes editors from *Jack and Jill, Child Life, Children's Digest, Highlights for Children, Wee Wisdom, Outdoor Life,* and *Boy Scout Manual.*

At the end of the course, the student/writer will have produced at least one publishable story - and they keep sending it back until it is. Furthermore, they offer marketing assistance for the writer's book and his magazine stories.

I do not consider the $680 fee too hefty at all for a two-year course. Besides the intensive instruction and critiquing, it includes ten instructional books, sent level-by-level as the writer progresses, and all return postage for as many returns as it takes to get it right.

I have to add that I have the world's greatest supporter. My husband let me quit my job, he bought me a computer, he encourages me to enroll in every creative writing course and workshop Chemeketa offers, and he's giving me two full years to be a student of writing. I know, I know, I'm a lucky lady.

Well-crafted mainstream fiction
is timeless, a sought-after property.
A concise, precise, witty guide
to fiction writing is Robert Newton Peck's
FICTION IS FOLKS: HOW TO CREATE UNFORGETTABLE CHARACTERS
(Writer's Digest Books)
Pay particular attention to his
"VANILLA PEOPLE"
and write for them.

HOW TO BE A TRENDY

If you want to sell what you write, you must write what sells.

And you must write it right now, and get it to market fast while fresh.

Remember the Ollie book? It hit the stands while the Colonel was still on the stand himself, and it was a hot seller for many days. But when Secretary Weinberger began telling his side of of the story, the North star waned and the hot seller became a hot potato.

Publishing is a trendy trade. "This year's hot seller may be next year's cold oatmeal," warns author Sheila Simonson.

Ellen Howard, award-winning author of juvenile books, agrees. She cites her book, *Gillyflower*, as an example. While she had no trouble getting in published (Atheneum Press), a friend with a book on the same topic could not get it accepted six months later.

Children's books in general are strong sellers and will continue to be. A 1987 issue of *Publishing Markets* reports: Retail sales of' children's books are booming and (are) expected to continue growing strongly for the next few years. Sales of children's hardcovers will rise 12.4% this year. Children's paperbacks will post a 13.1% increase."

While many book and magazine article topics are trendy and time-dated, "certain areas always sell," says agent Betsy Davidson of Pickering and Associates. "Celebrity books, a good diet book, a racy expose on corporations."

Another strong, steady seller: cookbooks. Several years ago tens of thousands of volumes were featured at a used-book fair in Eugene. The first day all the cookbooks were sold out and

Friends of the Library sent out a plea for more donations. In October 1987 Powell's Books in Portland opened a store featuring cookbooks - that's it, just cookbooks. In an interview on KXL Radio, store manager Heller Rathbone said they stock or can produce 26,000 titles - that's twenty-six thousand not volumes but titles. "People read cookbooks as reading material," Ms. Rathbone said. "They read for the information cookbooks contain about history, culture, and folkways. They read about eating out instead of actually eating out; they even read about regional and national cuisine as a substitute for traveling."

Best-selling cookbooks have a focus: a particular era, area, style (Cajun is big now, pasta was in 1985), or dietary specialty (beef is back). Fame sells: recipes of great chefs, of the stars, even cooking of the candidates.

Right now, in 1988, fame sells cookbooks and everything else. "The trend is celebrities. Celebrities sell magazines," says Redbook fiction editor Deborah Percell. Celebrities sell so well, she adds, that Redbook hopes to acquire short fiction by your favorite famous folks. However, she cautions writers hoping to break into Redbook not to try creating their own fiction *about* celebs.

In the Northwest we have two other perennial steady-moving genres: history and regional. "There are probably more serious historians per capita in Oregon and Washington than anywhere else in the country," says Elizabeth Mosher, manager of Polk County's historic Brunk House. "And regional books sell everywhere, in all kinds of outlets," says Eugene author Marje Blood, who's sold a lot of them herself.

Because the publishing industry deals with passing popularity, the writer's problem is obvious. If it's ebbtide for a topic, a publisher will pass; but they're not interested if you're years ahead of your time, either. Agents and publishers can't accurately predict what's going to capture the public next year, says New York agent John Pickering.

If the gurus of the industry can't tell what's going to sell, then your guess may be as good as theirs. Here are some ways you can educate your guesses.

Study *Forthcoming Books* (R. R. Bowker Company). It's a gigantic volume, in libraries, that lists every book that's been given an ISBN that will be published in a four-to-six-month period. Books are indexed by author, title, and subject. The subject listings indicate areas in which publishers have placed faith in the public's forthcoming preferences. Check the author listings, noting what topics the well-known, trendsetting writers are introducing . If M. Scott Peck brings up a new topic, you can be sure it will be a subject that sells.

Borrow your librarian's *Publisher's Weekly, Library Journal,* or other trade magazines. See what subjects are getting rave treatments. Books reviewed in these journals are, in the main, new or forthcoming releases, next month's news.

Read several issues of *Small Press*. Published by Meckler Corporation, it announces hundreds and reviews scores of new and forthcoming releases. The small presses of America are trend-setters, willing to do and say what major publishers don't want to risk. Small and independent presses don't worry about being ahead of the wave; they like to be first.

Contact magazine editors. Ask what general topics they will address in coming months.

Keep abreast of demographics. Then humanize the data. Today's sociological statistics are tomorrows's issues. And tomorrow's readers.

Finally, brethren, if your idea isn't ready yet for people, write it anyway. Polish it, complete it, then put it away for its time. Someday, suddenly, a single event may make your manuscript a timely, hot commodity.

Remember that piece you thought you'd write, that satire of organized religion? That nobody would touch? Don't you wish you'd done it anyway? Then, when Tammy Bakker dropped her first tear, you'd whip it out and you'd be the first in line with this suddenly stylish subject.

WHAT TO WRITE? . . . WHAT THEY READ!

John Kremer in BOOK MARKETING UPDATE NEWSLETTER, Feb. 88. Gallup Poll:

Women. . .buy 59% of all books
buy 72% of books given as gifts
in 1986, 81% of women bought cookbooks
71% bought children's books
69% bought health/diet/fitness
92% bought romances
79% bought kid fic
79% bought contemporary fiction
55% bought humor

Men. . . . . . 82% bought financial--economics
52% bought home--garden
66% bought Western fiction
60% bought science fiction
60% -- action/adventure novels

MARILYN JOHNSON,
Phoenix Writer's Service:

What's selling?
Just about everything.
There's a vast variety out there. Any topic that's written well is likely to find a home.

KAREN SUE DUNCAN, Editorial Director,
Manuscripts International:

Vietnam, for instance, was in, then out, then in again when the movies appeared.

The timing was right, so Duncan prioritized to complete editing Nebraska author JOHN D'ARCY's **The Death Game.**
The timing was perfect, too, for JACK ESTES' **Fields of Innocence**, a Vietnam chronicle written before the genre's popular peak and ready for the stands at just the precise moment.

Sue Henry, conference facilitator:

In analyzing small press journals' current reviews and announcements of new and forthcoming books, I see some new in's: No-diet diets, No-exercise exercises, and spoofs of pop-psych help-yourself. I see a switch from do-it-yourself manuals to directories of Who-Does-It-For-You.

And from politicians' hijinx this year, political satire just has to boom in 1989. . . I wish I'd completed my self-help satire and started my political roast.

KiKi Canniff:

. .And if yours is a current or oncoming topic, don't waste its 2 or 3 best marketing years waiting around for a big publisher.
Publish it yourself.

AND DON'T THROW ANYTHING AWAY

SCRIPTWRITING

It isn't just for New York and California any more. Playwriting as a genre has taken a center-stage spotlight in the Northwest and, like writers of children's literature, Northwest scriptcrafters are being sought out by the big ones.

Northwest authors' works have appeared on stage all along. *The Egg and I, One Flew Over the Cuckoo's Nest, The Deer Hunter, The Equalizer, Clan of the Cave Bear.* But those were works that were adapted; now the playwrights per se are having their day. Portlander Tad Savinar's *Talk Radio* plays in Manhattan. Springfield's Dorothy Velasco's *Oregon Fever* goes to Independence, Missouri, the "other end" of the trail.

And other Northwesterners gain notice as scripters for the stage and for screens of both kinds: Judy GeBauer, Sharon Glantz, Carl Sander, Nancy Klementowski, Michael Whelan, Sharon Whitney, Karen Karbo . . .

Northwest Playwrights Guild, P.O. Box 95259, Seattle 98145, serves the five Northwest states. Originated in 1986, it sponsors competitions and readings, produces a newsletter, publishes a regional theatre directory. In summer of 1987, the Oregon chapter was formed and by November it had fifty members. Contact: Sharon Whitney, 2460 Greenway Drive N.E., Salem 97301.

There are growing opportunities for playwrights to study, read their works, and to be performed here, far from the maddening crowd.

SESSION 4

BEING ADVISED

PANEL: What Editors Say

SYMPOSIUM: What Writers Say

WHAT EDITORS SAY

We asked 32 editors of regional and national periodicals to comment on several topics relating to freelancers and their submissions. Nine responded - about the expected rate of reply from any selected lot of inquiries.

Their answers are points we writers would do well to take seriously.

WHAT BUGS YOU ABOUT WRITERS AND SUBMISSIONS?

Naomi Woolever, National Grit:
"A writer who is so enthralled with his own prose that, upon rejection of his manuscript, he writes a scathing letter to the editor for having returned his copy. Fortunately there are few of these. Professionals accept rejections gracefully." *(Worth noting: Woolever uses the grammatical "his" in reference to indefinite he or she. If you submit to Grit, do the same.)*

Adele Mallot, Friendly Exchange
"My most important advice to writers starts with reading - reading the publication the writer wants to work for, the guidelines it offers, the letters sent by the editor. When the magazine has never published an article about Europe, why would a writer waste time promoting a piece about European beaches? When the magazine has never published a first-person article, why would a

writer think his/her first-person article would be the one to change that policy?

"Next, listen. When there is a go ahead from the editor, write the article assigned, not the one you want to write.

"And third, don't be afraid to say ' no' to an editor. No, if the editor is giving you too little time to do the work. No, if the article is outside your field of expertise.

"One other off-the-wall thought. Do not submit a new idea each week to one editor, if that editor is in charge of an annual or quarterly. An editor can use only so much material from one writer. There has to be a balance of information, style, and texture in a publication and to achieve that, many editors want to use a variety of writers. In my case, I buy some 40-50 manuscripts a year that will be published in four issues. Some writers submit queries so regularly I could fill all my editorial needs by working with one writer. Pace your queries so that your ideas will not be rejected simply because of space/issue availability."

Verle Bell, Wee Wisdom

"(1) I object to being sent an extensive bio-sheet from an author, filling me with the expectations that the enclosed will be the answer to my prayers for something true-to-life, attention-captivating, and easy for our grade-school readers to read, only to find it sounds as though it had been ground through a dusty mill. Often talented novices come through with more fresh, inspired ideas than often-published pros.

"(2) I find most offensive . . . writing that is overdone in its abundance of adjectives, adverbs, contrived verbs, all conspiring to present an artificial tone. We do, after all, have a juvenile readership.

"(3) Another pitfall for writers to avoid is the use of disconnected thoughts. Small children need to have thoughts and plots clearly delineated - and fun to read.

"(4) We are limited to 800 words, and dislike having to cut an otherwise good story down from 1200 or more. Our writers need to read *Wee Wisdom's* guidelines - and to study the magazine."

Charles M. Jonak, Kiwanis

"Their failure to take suggestions and an apparent indifference to the magazine's style, needs, etc."

Ruralite

"Rewrite should be a writer's Ten Commandments. He/she should send for guidelines and rewrite according to them, and strive to match the writing style of the target magazine. Stilted, ponderous 'journalese' is the mark of an amateur. Most writers fail because they feel they 'know how to write', and make no real effort to start over with each new article. Good writing on a poor story idea is so much wasted effort."

Pat Vargas, Gurney's Gardening News

"- Missed deadlines: You can be early but never late.

- Failure to read my publication. This causes submissions on unsuitable topics, writing at the wrong level of language, and inappropriate article length.

- Failure to submit photos/graphics as promised.

- Poor leads.

- On several occasions I've had to pull articles a week before press date because the same article appeared in a competing publication. I buy first rights. I always call the editor of the other pub. When this happens, that writer is not likely to sell to either of us again. If I can't trust the writer on this very basic issue, how can I believe what he says in his article?

--Don't make errors of fact. Look it up. Verify. Then double check yet again."

A WRITER RECEIVES A GO AHEAD, BUT THE FINISHED PIECE IS RETURNED WITH "DOES NOT MEET OUR NEEDS." THE GO AHEAD OBVIOUSLY INDICATES THE TOPIC AND THE PROPOSED CONTENT AND ANGLE DID IN FACT FIT THE NEED. SOMETHING ELSE IS AT FAULT. WHY MIGHT AN INITIAL GO AHEAD RESULT IN A FINAL REJECTION?

"Because a well-written, tempting query may be followed up by an utterly crappy story."

"The idea was good. The written article was not focused clearly, and organization was poor. Or, although the query promised something new and different, the material was material we'd already covered."

"Poor writing. Inadequate research."

"Sometimes the information is poorly researched - the article contains little more than was in the query. Sometimes, the writing is poor - no interesting little anecdotes, poor style. Sometimes the writer ignores my length requirements and I don't have time to rewrite it."

"There are two basic reasons I reject a finished piece after an initial go-ahead: poor research that does not support the query's premise or poor writing that demolishes a good query. There may be other reasons such as a magazine changing its approach or focus, or budgetary considerations that come into play late in the year. There is one other factor and that is the question of rights to be purchased. Our guidelines indicate rights to be purchased. But after a query gets a go-ahead, I've had writers try to change the rights they will sell. As an editor, I have only one voice in setting policy within a company and I can't change the established policy for one individual."

"A lead that doesn't grab. If I can fix it quickly, I do; if not, it's rejected."

"The story that does not fit our writing style is rejected. Our pieces all follow the same style, as though written by the same author. If a submission doesn't follow that style, we don't use it."

"Good writing has organization, clarity, punch. Anecdotes are essential. If a query shows promise, we give a go-ahead; if the piece doesn't deliver, we reject."

The vice president of one of North America's largest book printers, an East Coast firm, said:

"The real distinction of a vanity publisher is the quality of writing. You wouldn't believe some of the *garBAHge* that comes to us passed off as publishable work. Especially poetry. Bad poetry is worse than a bad novel.
Serious, professional small publishers have their manuscripts edited. Vanity authors believe their every word too sacred to change."

Robert Miles, R & E Miles Publishing:

A book manuscript needs an editor, period. An author, no matter how well he writes, needs that third-person eye to see the manuscript from a distance. And one should have an editor other than a spouse or offspring, regardless of their competence.

"The best part of a writers conference is hearing what other writers have to say."

WHAT WRITERS SAY

JOURNALIST, OREGON

Be glad you turned down the job as reporter on the daily news. They edit, cut, and don't publish half your copy. You're not allowed to be very creative. I've been with them for 17 years and it's been very frustrating.

JOURNALIST, IDAHO

I enjoy journalism. I know what I write will be published, and at $2.50 an inch, that's better than most writers do in a month. And it's steady.

KEN BOLF, OREGON

Most of those little books of poetry are read by other poets. Poets have a very supportive, non-competitive network.

AUDREY THOMPSON, WASHINGTON

Once I cut a 2700-word piece down to 1800. It lost none of its substance.

SUNNI SENJIM

For a while I worked on my novel early in the morning, before going to work. It was no good. I couldn't shake it off for hours; I couldn't come back.

ANDI ZYLSCHA

While I'm writing fiction, I AM those characters.' It's difficult for me to come back to the real world to cook dinner.

GAIL O'MALLEY

I no longer smoke while I work. Computers are too expensive to smoke around. By next April I'll have quit.

JOYCE THOMPSON

The computer has saved more lungs than the Heart Association and Cancer Societies combined.

GARY F. SMITH

My publisher ordered a revision of my 400-page book. With my word processor, I had it done in 48 working hours.

Hi-tek has circled full 'round: your old electric is again the latest advancement. Through laseroptics, your ***edited, error-free*** *typed manuscript can be typeset directly from your page. At a shade less cost than to reformat a disk into typeset and el mucho greato less than to keyboard it again. . . Now you can get into desktop publishing without having to get into desktop publishing.*

Information today is plentiful, accessible, and cheap. Most colleges have access to scores of data banks and can get information quickly. Marylhurst College, for example, provided four pages of factual article summaries together with bibliographical references to please the most meticulous scientific editor. All the data needed for three articles on three different topics. For $20.

But computers don't know everything. The one used to typeset this book, for instance, doesn't know how to make a dash. So we had to delete the sermon on punctuation--the one that rants and stomps and yells, "A hyphen is not a punctuation mark!"
And, oh, yes, the next time you do this, tell your typesetter to please don't erase the disc before your final proofreading.

FORMER EDITOR, Regional Weekly:

You should see the editing we do on
that woman's copy!! She's a stringer
in another state, she gets all the news and
she gets the facts right. At $50 an article,
she makes $300 a week. The only thing she
doesn't do right is write, so we keep her.
Don't think for a minute that writing
skill is all it takes for newswriting.

KARLENE BOYD, Review Editor:

Is there a correlation
between neatness and mechanics
and skillfully crafted writing?
Absolutely.
When a manuscript comes in here,
I can tell by looking at it whether
it's going to be well-written.
I'm hardly ever wrong.

YVONNE ROTHERT, Fiction Editor,
Northwest Magazine:

I'll change the passive verbs to active.

EDITOR OF A SMALL PRESS and INDEPENDENT FREELANCE EDITOR:

When an author brought me a manuscript I asked, "Who's your reader?" "Oh, everyone," she answered cheerfully, "everyone will want to read it." She doesn't know the second thing about book authoring: there isn't a book for everyone. Even the world's all-time best-seller is not read by more than 5% of the world's people. When I see a manuscript I want to know who it's for. Very few small press books are sold in big stores; an author must identify his audience and identify the specific means available to sell the books outside the circle of chains . . . The lady has a hell of a story, but a metaphysical science fiction is not, either, for "everyone."

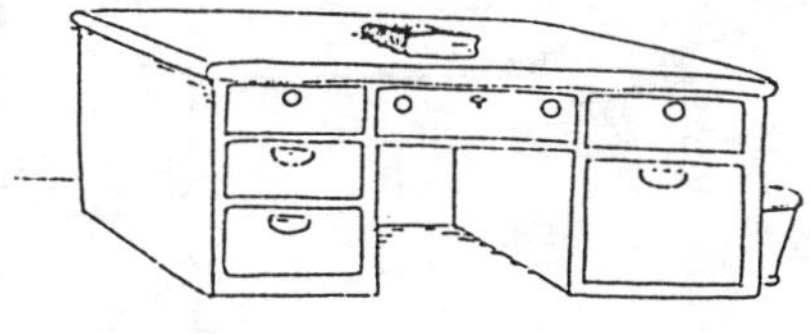

To force his eighth graders to write with motion and sparkle, teacher JACK McGARVEY banned the use of is, are, was, were--not only in the kids' written work but in their classroom speech as well. In an article reported in November/December 1987 *Learning* magazine, McGarvey describes his procedure, the kids' experiences, and illustrates some of the outstanding improvements in their use of language. While attending to his freelancing, he told his computer to search his own work and beep all his forbidden words. "When I rewrote those sentences, I found I used fewer words and turned more to my thesaurus. I've never written in a more careful, disciplined way," he wrote.

And, oh, yes - in the author's bionote, *Learning* notes:

"Jack McGarvey teaches . . . in Coleytown Middle School, Westport, Conn., and IS a freelance writer."

SESSION 5

BEING REPRESENTED

How to Get an Agent

Book Proposals

Self-Publishing

Your Arts Council

HOW TO GET AN AGENT

"Get an agent." - M. K. Wren, author of six mystery novels and an armload of others.

"Get an agent." - Sheila Simonson, poet and author of seven Regency romances.

"Don't just get an agent. Get a shark. A business person; not one who understands the thematic points of literary art . . . When you write to an agent, don't try to be cute." - Karen Karbo, screenwriter.

"Our prime concern is salability. We are in the marketing business. Artistic and aesthetic qualities are only secondary concerns, if at all." - John Pickering, agent.

"Most publishers won't look at anything that doesn't come through an agent." --Dan Levant, Madrona Publishing.

"Eager to work with new writers...prefers working with published/established writers..." Agent listing, *Writer's Market* .

"Works with established authors who have published one or more books." - Agent listing.

"Publishers want agented writers. Agents don't want writers who haven't been published. How can you get out of a bind like that?" - Thousands of writers.

"One way into an agent's office is to be recommended by an author the agent already represents," says a Washington writer who found his agent that way.

"So how do I get to know these published authors?" asks a workshop participant.

You can make yourself known to an established writer by taking a course or a workshop he teaches - many, many writers do this, privately or through colleges. If it's a class of long duration, the writer-instructor becomes acquainted with you and your work. If it's a one or two day shot, present yourself to your instructor, talk about your work completed and in progress. In either case, be prepared to present some work you hope to publish. Request a critique, schedule a conference, invite him to dinner, proposition him - do anything to gain his notice; then strike.

You can become acquainted through writers' organizations. Not only are those groups sources of information, inspiration, support, and a literary identity for members, but they provide valuable, steady contacts.

Writers who have no connections through an agent's client study Literary Agents listings in writers' publications. *Writer's Market, Writer's Yellow Pages and Literary Marketplace* carry such listings.

Eugene author Marje Blood suggests that writers who are shopping identify agencies in the listings who "work with new authors" or "accept new clients." Then begin sending queries.

"When you query an agent, send a resume," says Marje, whose own resume is so long she had to reduce it to fit it on a page. She lists the customary education and work experience (most writers have jobs!), her business endeavors (she owns a literary service and her own publishing firm), plus her writing-related activities and publication credits. Marje lists publications which have carried her articles because they are well-known and high-paying ones; "but if you've not written for big-timers you needn't list the names of the publications," she says to agent - seekers.

Those publication credits are all-important, say writers who have crossed an agent's threshold.

"If you plan to take a novel to a publisher, get yourself a track record of short story publishing first," advises Joyce Thompson, who's done a lot of both.

"If you plan to take anything at all to an agent, get yourself a track record by publishing anything at all first," adds Gail Tycer.

How to get those publication credits? Some freelancing for a fee, some contributions for free--being in training, paying your dues, just like we discussed in Session 2 of this conference.

There is another direction to an agent's door. A firm in Dayton, Washington (Manuscripts International, 408 East Main Street, Dayton 99328) specializes in editing and polishing short and novel-length manuscripts to publication perfection, and then submitting them, upon the author's instruction, to an agent. They do it for a fee, of course, which depends upon the amount of work required; but overall their cost is quite a bit less than the usual $5 per page to $25 per hour charged by other editorial services. The firm guarantees agency placement although they can't promise publication--nobody can; and if they do, walk away. Nevertheless, R.G. Williscroft, Ph.D, the firm's president, boasts the industry's best track record in getting first novels published. The Dayton manuscript service also places single short stories with an agent.

Phoenix Writer's Service, 57 Main Street, SH 8119, Littlefork, MN 56653 is an agent. Phoenix maintains a database of members' writing and editors' needs. Pieces that have been completed and are awaiting marketing are noted, as well as each writer's experience, fields of interest, fields of specialty, and the like, so that editors can choose writers for assignments. Phoenix does the footwork of handling your queries for you. They handle fiction, articles, poetry, and dramascripts.

For members, the service maintains a toll-free number which they encourage writers to use endlessly for up - to - the - day information about current market needs, editorial requests, contests, grants, and awards. With daily updated information, writers of course have access to editors' needs now. Compare that to national magazines whose submission-to-print lag for "updates" is as long as four months.

"For publication credits, the best way is regionals," says Marje Blood. She means articles in regional periodicals. She means books with regional focus.

Are we back to books? To publishing a book before a publisher wants to publish your book?

"That's right," Marje says. You get a track record so you can get an agent so you can get your novel to a publisher. A novel is a long-term goal.

"So how do I get my regional book published?" asks the workshop participant.

"Publish it yourself," says Marje.

"You form your own business and you publish your own work and you prove you can sell what you write," says Kiki Canniff, whose company, K-2 Enterprises, publishes her heavy-seller regionals.

So the author who has no agent might find one through a recommendation, through a literary service's referral, or by hustling one up through the inquiry route. Or, as more and more are doing now, by publishing his own book.

If you do go agent-shopping, you'll wonder whether to go to an established agent with famous clients, or to a hungry one just getting started.

Says agent Aaron Priest, Erma Bombeck's man, "You've got to go to somebody who's looking for business."

BOOK PROPOSALS

"The book proposal is as important as the book itself," Naomi Miller Stokes told an Oregon Writers' Colony conference.

"Maybe more," said OWC member Jean Auel. "I spent two weeks writing and rewriting my proposal for *Clan*."

"Proposal?" The author of a manuscript-returned-home was perplexed. "I know about synopsis outline summary query, but I've never heard of proposal."

The proposal is the crucial item of book salesmanship, particularly critical if you're just introducing your work to a publisher or agent. It's also a step many authors with first book manuscripts don't know about. A book proposal is very different from the article proposal discussed in Session 3. It's the toughest thing you'll ever write, and you'll need guidelines from an expert.

How to Write a Book Proposal by Michael Larson (Writer's Digest Books) is a no-fooling-around, step-by-step guide. Another clear, succinct how-to is in John Boswell's *The Awful Truth About Publishing.*

Larson and Boswell show authors each step and explain why they are necessary. The advantages of composing a book proposal are that it forces the author to develop a clear focus, to organize and outline specifically and coherently, and to assess the marketability of the book. As Larson points out, the proposal requires the author to state precisely who the audience is, how that readership can be reached, and what's in the book for the reader.

A friend, an awesome-lot published writer from my old home grounds in Pacific County,

Washington, told me that a sample proposal needs to be placed . . . right about . . . here. It isn't here. In the first place, a proposal written according to Larson's formula requires some 25 to 35 double-spaced pages for a 14-chapter nonfiction . . . and you'll find better samples in the two books cited.

In the second place you wouldn't want to read a proposal I made up, anyway. See, I wrote a couple of them, two different books . . . followed all the directions exactly as Michael Larson said to do to create a winning proposal . . . sent them to Larson, expecting he'd want to be my agent . . .and got them back with the winning phrase of the trade: Doesn't Work For Me.

ALYCE CORNYN-SELBY, business communications consultant, author, publisher, to a publishers'/authors' seminar:

Your book must focus on your readers, on their concerns, on what they need. Your book must fill their needs and solve their problems.

Your promotional material must not highlight you the author but the reader looking for solutions. Identify your readers and identify exactly what's in this book for them. Tell them what problems you address and present solutions clearly. And be brief--most 200-page books could say it in 43.

Alyce identifies her own area of specialty: "I write for business people addressing personnel and management concerns. I write books for people who don't have time to read books."

Cornyn-Selby's TAKE YOUR HANDS OFF MY ATTITUDE--YOUR RIGHT TO A BAD ATTITUDE: THE ONLY REMAINING HOPE FOR SANITY IN THE SERVICE INDUSTRIES measures 4½ x 5½", is 43 pages, has but two sentences per page.

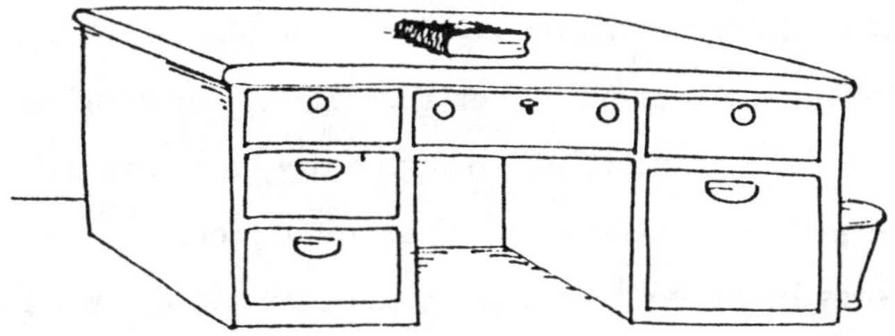

SELF PUBLISHING

Even if you have not considered self-publishing your own book(s) you owe it to your overall professionalism to know something about the fastest-growing segment of the literary industry.

Only a decade or so ago, authors who published their own work were scorned by the trade. Writers who would pay a printer to manufacture a book, it was believed, were only those whose writing was so bad a "legit" publisher wouldn't buy it. Vanity presses were looked down on, as were the books they produced and the authors who wrote them.

Boy, how things change!

In 1987, there were "about 20,000" small and independent presses and the number grows weekly, literally, according to John Kremer of Ad-Lib Publications. Kremer is one of the leading figures in North American self-publishing and Ad-Lib is a premiere and primo independent press. Publishers Marketing Association, an independent press marketing co-op based at Hermosa Beach, California, had, in mid-1987, nearly 600 publisher members. In Oregon alone, Northwest Association of Book Publishers' membership approaches 200.

There are some distinctions between "vanity" publishing and self-publishing/independent presses, although those in the publishing industry do not themselves agree precisely where and what the delineation is.

1988 Writer's Market ignores "self-publishing" altogether; but then, that book is for freelancers and not intended to be a self-publisher's guide. The entry "Vanity publisher" reads: See *subsidy publisher . . . Subsidy publisher. A book publisher who charges the author for the cost to typeset and print his book, the jacket, etc., as opposed to a royalty publisher that pays the author.*" The book unabashedly advises writers considering subsidy publishing to request their cautionary information.

"The difference is that a vanity publisher pays someone else to design, edit, and produce the book," says Dimi Press owner- author-publisher Dick Lutz, president of Northwest Association of Book Publishers. Then, after reflecting thoughtfully, he amends, "That really doesn't explain it, does it? I hire experts to do those technical things, too."

"When one self-publishes he undertakes the entire enterprise as a publisher," says Dennis Stovall of Media Weavers. (I'm going out on the limb of opinion that Stovall, a freelancer, author, editor, reviewer, consultant to writers and independent presses, instructor of workshops and seminars, and a publisher, is far and away the single most outstanding total literary figure in the Northwest as I write this - when 1988 is in diapers. And I don't say this because we're drinking buddies, either; I don't think Dennis would recognize me if we met in the checkout line.) Stovall continues, "A self-publisher/independent publisher/small press (terms often used interchangeably, although Publishers Marketing Association president Robert E. Alberti of Impact Publishers cringes at such an all-in-one definition) is a business."

"A business for profit," adds the office manager of a profitable publisher. "Not so," contends John Kremer , a profitable publisher. "A vanity book may or may not be produced as a business enterprise, and many self-publishers know their book won't make big bucks, either." In fact, the major houses freely admit that only a few of their books are money-makers, and those titles pay the way for the rest. So profitability or not isn't a valid differention between vanity or not.

Kremer, who modestly claims his is a small press (he's made it a big business, guys), continues, "A self-publisher has to look at himself as a publisher and a promoter, especially a promoter. Vanity presses don't promote. Independent presses do."

But to promote or not isn't a clear line of demarcation, either. Juanita Matheson-Ferry (Afcom Publishing), in an article in *Publishing Northwest,* said, "After working with an agent and publishers for 20 years, I got tired of their nitpicking and lack of promotion." M.K. Wren, author of eight or nine novels from a major publisher and holder of many awards for her writing, told a symposium audience, "My publisher doesn't promote its mid-line. I do." Agent Michael Larson tells authors that their book proposals must include "What YOU will do to promote your book." And New York agent John Pickering concurs, "Publishers expect you to take an active role in promoting your book." Said Nancy Hedberg, "Neither of my publishers did much to promote my books."

At a conference of librarians and independent publishers held at Salem Public Library in February, 1987, a librarian who purchases for a public library in a Southwest Washington city cleared a lot of fog when she explained it. "If the spine and verso page says Vantage Press or Exposition Press, I won't buy it. If the same book - same cover, same everything else - is from something like Jones Publishing,and has Jones' ISBN (International Standard Book Number) and a CIP (Library of Congress Cataloging in Publication number), I'd probably buy it, particularly if it's by a regional author."

Added another acquisitions librarian, "If there's a decent review in *Library Journal* or in *Publisher's Weekly*, I'll certainly buy it." The double-catch here is that trade journals won't review a book from Vantage but they might if it's from Jones Publishing.

Independent presses/self-publishers establish themselves in the industry by procuring those numbers that make their books "real" and "official" - and purchasable, and by having their titles listed in trade publications. They establish themselves as legal businesses by registering a business name, Jones Publishing or whatever, with their state department of commerce, they pay taxes, and promote their wares. For an author - publisher to institute his own business is no more a matter of vanity than for a painter or potter to open a shop, for Lionel Richie to establish his own recording company, or for Niki, Microsoft, or Apple to sell what they create. Why should authors be the only segment of American free enterprise to be called vain?

Independent presses have arrived in credibility, respectability, and visibility. Numerous trade journals specialize in spotlighting the works of small presses; trade fairs and conventions exhibit and promote their books; marketing cooperatives serve as informational clearinghouses and enable self-publishers to catalog, advertise, and promote their wares effectively and economically.

While the number of small presses soars, the "big houses" dwindle. Depending on how they define "major publishers", the experts who author the small press journals have recently figured the big publishers at 8, and at 20. However it's calculated, the major houses number far fewer than independent presses.

There are many reasons why authors choose to publish their own work. The most obvious, no doubt, is that authors are unable to place a manuscript with a major house, so they go into business for themselves. This leaves the impression that S-P books must not be otherwise publishable, and in some cases it's true. Despite the immense gains of a decade, many in the distributing and buying end of the industry still look askance at S-P books, and enough bad stuff is out there to furnish reason for their opinion. But every industry has its culls: accountants make errors, farmers produce poor hay, and some bakers cook up cakes you can't choke down.

But there's an error in the chip if it says self-publishers are also-rans. Mark Twain and Edgar Rice Burroughs published their own, and so did Thomas Paine, Ben Franklin, and Moses. Barbara Harris (Barbara Harris, Inc.) has sold over 700,000 copies of *Let's Cook Microwave*. Mickey Hickman's *Homer, the Country Boy* sold $10,000 worth in its first three weeks out, and negotiations for movie rights were underway within six months. Harriett L. Smith (Smith, Smith, & Smith Publishing Co.) has 12 titles, Paulette Jarvey (Hot off the Press, Inc.), more than 50. Helene Sawyer's *Cooking with Gourmet Mustards* (Culinary Arts, Ltd.)

went to its second printing even before it was released. J. Wesley Sullivan's second book (Nauvillus Press) was on its way less than a year after his first.

A second reason compliments the first. Many fine manuscripts aren't accepted because traditional major houses publish what they calculate will sell nationally and to the masses. In general, that rules out local and regional books, those for a specific narrow readership, chapbooks - poetry particularly - and anything that doesn't fit the New York mold. "They told me I had to put some steamy scenes in my novel," a Klamath Falls author told me, "even though that doesn't fit the story, the characters, or my style."

Another genre receiving little support in "major" circles is literary fiction. "For really fine quality short fiction of high literary calling, look to the little mags," says Tom Ferte. Margurita Donnelley, an editor at Calyx, told a librarians' conference that the big publishers aren't willing to risk doing much good literature; yet her press has won awards for literary excellence.

Many self-publishers are experienced authors with prior sales. Juanita Matheson-Ferry (Afcom Publishing) is one. Her fifth book is in production in her own house as this is being written.

Paula Montgomery (Monte Publishing): "Editors deleted my best phrases. They cut off the text when they used up a page. I'll never go through another commercial house."

Neither will Helen Hecker, Vancouver USA writer whose Twin Peaks Press has published no fewer than seven titles. When she was president of Northwest Association of Book Publishers she told the membership, "You can go to a commercial publisher as a last resort, I guess. I wouldn't."

The chance to keep a greater share of profits if any, is one reason self-publishers do so. Don't misunderstand, though. The expenses are plenty and the risks even greater. Just as in any business.

Authors like having the total control of their work that self - publishing gives them. They like the turn - around time. With a conventional royalty sale, authors look at a year and a half to two years from submission to book shelf. With S-P, it's a lot closer to an immediate reward - three to four months. And that will be a big plus if the tax law retains the clause that says writers can not deduct expenses incurred in their writing until their writing is actually marketed.

Producing and marketing your own work isn't all sunshine and flowers. It's a financial and artistic risk. You become less an artist and more a promoter, which many writers simply can't make themselves do. But it can be very satisfying and worthwhile, and you may want to look at it.

SELF-PUBLISHING?

HERE ARE YOUR HOMEWORK ASSIGNMENTS

BOOK MARKETING MADE EASIER, John Kremer. Ad-Lib Publications, P.O. Box 1102, Fairfield, Iowa 52556. $14.95 + $1.00 p&h.

COMPLETE GUIDE TO SELF PUBLISHING, Marilyn and Tom Ross. About Books, Inc., Box 538, Saguache, OH 81149. $21.95 ppd.

SELF-PUBLISHING CONSULTANTS
Publishers Book Works
1415 S.E. 8th Ave., Portland, OR 97214

Ki-2 Enterprises
P.O. Box 13322, Portland, OR 97213

Dennis Stovall
Rt. 3 Box 376, Hillsboro, OR 97214

Dennis Stovall tells this vanity horror story.

A Florida press offered to print 3000 copies of a book for $16,000,but they would bind (affix cover on) only 60 copies. The author would assume ownership of 30 copies. That's right: For sixteen thou, he got 30 copies of his own book. But . . . he was given the "right" to BUY more copies at the regular bookstore discount. (Bookstores buy for 40% off the regular cover price.)

To "promote" the book, Florida put two classified ads in print media. Then, if the book did not sell x number of copies, the author would have the privilege of purchasing the remainders.

Dennis adds, "A 'publishing service' in Washington state is hustling people with lots of bucks."

YOUR ARTS COUNCIL

Used to be, THE ARTS meant painting and sculpture, theatre like Ibsen, the Greeks, and opera; and chamber music. Then, "they" categorized them all lumpy as Fine Arts and Performing Arts and the arts community recognized all who created with their hand and did their thing for an assembled audience.

Then a new artform stirred and emerged. Somewhere in the dust stacks of a library and the musty office of a state arts commission, someone realized that writing was creative, too, and the new artform was called Literary Arts. As far as I can tell, it happened in the Eighties, and Oregon was on the edge. Don't take that as gospel, because I was in Alaska at the time and one thing The Great Land has always done is to recognize all creativity as artform, whether it be crafting hunting implements of ivory, sewing fur garments with a bone needle, or composing poetry of ten words.

Oregon Arts Commission and Oregon State Library, thanks to Peter Sears of the former and Wes Doak of the latter, moved, shook, and supported support of the writing community until the idea breathed and lived. Now each Northwest state has a Council of the Arts or an Arts Commission; most areas have regional Councils, and each promotes the literary arts more and more.

Arts commissions award grants, stipends, scholarships, and literary awards. State libraries publish *Oregon Authors* or *Washington Authors*, annual directories cheering and promoting writers who've published books during the previous year; furthermore, the library maintains a clip file for authors, collecting reviews, news, and press releases about each author and his books. This year (1988) Oregon Arts Commission-Oregon State Library publishes *The Oregon Small Presses and Literary Magazine Catalogue.*

Northwest Literary Calendar, a monthly listing begun in 1986, announces events of all sizes in all locations, from Bumbershoot to Association of Northwest Writers conferences to meetings of Skagit Valley Writers Group to a poetry reading at Billings library. If your library or literary group would like one, send your request to Michael Polacek, Oregon Arts Commission, 835 Summer Street, Salem, Or 97301.

Bainbridge Island Arts Council publishes an annual Northwest Poets and Artists Calendar, a full-color slick featuring twelve poets and twelve artists. Selections are from juried competition. For contest information and to order, contact Bainbridge Island Arts Council, 8949 Fletcher Bay Rd, Bainbridge, WA 98110. Director Nancy Rekow is at 206-842-4855. Many areas publish regional newsletters or periodical tabloids of arts news. You'll probably find one at your library, in music stores, and even at banks.

Sears reports momentum supporting literary arts occurring in Idaho and Montana, where arts commissions are growing active and vital. And it's my patriotic duty to report that those entities are patterning their service and activities after the manner of their coastal neighbors.

For the support your state Arts Commission and regional Councils of the Arts give you, we urge you to support them. Get in touch . . . discover what they can do for you. And, please, reciprocate. That means donate - a contribution which will come back full and running over.

GENERAL SESSION

CONFERENCE WRAPPER

Brass, Hustle, and Grit

BRASS, HUSTLE AND GRIT

"Do you mean if your piece gets published, someone else's doesn't?" Bob asked, incredulous.

"Well . . . yeah."

"Gee. That's a bugger." He's a marshmallow heart; instead of cheering for the victor he grieves the loser, unless the victor's name is Seahawks. "So if they print your story, does that mean it was better than someone else's?"

"Maybe not. It might mean I got there first, or thumped my drum the loudest."

You see, the potential product of the writer is absolutely limitless. Tens of thousands of writers, hundreds of thousands of pieces of copy, and more of both every day. If you don't write it, someone else will. But the market - the number of publiations, the space available, the number of readers and the money they have to spend on their habit...those are finites.

Talent and technicianship aren't enough. Writing to publish also requires brass, hustle, and grit.

Let's talk about grit first, because if you don't have that - that tenacity fed by goal-mindedness and belief in yourself - talent and hustle won't make you much difference.

Let this be your first number - one primo guiding overriding principle: Don't believe 'em if it ain't nice and don't let 'em grind you down.

You've heard of Albert Einstein? The kid his first grade teacher said was backward and his fifth grade teacher flunked? Or Napoleon Bonaparte, the epileptic dyslexic? Or Erma Bombeck, who couldn't find a publisher or an agent until . . . Or Margaret Mitchell, who received rejection slips from 32 publishers before . . .

When I taught school, every day I confronted students who had gotten the idea that they, youngsters of a culturally "different" minority, were dumb. They called themselves that. I spent my days cheering, supporting, applauding them. While other teachers spoke of the kids' vegetative state, I never gave up on the vegetables in English One. And they never let me down. My most frequently-played rerun: You Can.

I knew from experience they could. Let me tell you about a youngster named Susan.

Her third grade teacher told Susan she was not bright; sixth grade, she had no musical talent; high school, she'd never learn to type; her college comp prof, she couldn't write. Most youngsters shatter under a continual barrage of negatives, but not Susan. She just felt sorry for all those critics who didn't know much. Those were the forties and fifties, when "positive image" was called conceit, when it was not okay to say you're okay. But the youngster possessed a sense of self-confidence, you see. She didn't know about pop-psych so the buzzwords didn't get in the way.

She didn't worry about the gloomy prognostications but hung on to the encouragements of other, more optimistic cheerleaders and the successes they catylized, successes like writing for the hometown weekly, winning music scholarships, and graduating from college with honors.

She applied these lessons to her students, and then again to herself when she began to write. Of rejections she philosophizes that a flop is not a permanent state.

So the first ingredient for being a writer is that gritty conviction that you can. But after the "can" must come "do", and that's where you need the hustle.

Throughout this conference, writers of status, working pros, have told us that editors are starving for copy, and that if you write well, you'll sell. My remark about the finite nature of places and spaces does not negate theirs, for the truth is that although there are thousands of writers, many don't get "a round tuit" - they don't DO it.

Examples. I told the writers in a workshop to send me a manuscript for a free critique and none did. A newsletter's marketing update noted a Willamette Valley monthly seeks paid copy and none was submitted. A daily paper went out begging, literally and with effort, for a correspondent at $3.50 an inch, up to $800 a month, and after three months they still were begging. For no less than three weeks a university to my south advertised for a writer-editor for its PR department, while a college to my north hunted for one for a month. A classified "Writer-collaborator-ghost writer wanted" ran for two months in a writer's newsletter. A contest announced nationally in no fewer than twelve publications received seven entries. A bimonthly with a circulation of 31,000 for six months announced they would publish poetry and short stories submitted by readers, and they received . . . one . . . poem. SAIFCO ran an ad for a writer-editor for so long it was practically ongoing. The Oregon Arts Commission has grants awaiting writers who ask for them and the grants still wait to be asked for, says a spokesperson for the commission.

Where IS everybody and when are you going to DO it?

Well, hustle is by no means limited to watching the papers. It's also marketing. Marketing your skills and the products of your skills. With grit.

"I have 35 submissions out all the time," says Jeff Taylor. "A dozen queries and articles out all the time," says Tom Bannan. "More assignments than I can handle," said Gail O'Malley.

A Vancouver novelist revised her book five times and then submitted it to a publisher. When it came back, she said with cheerful determination, "I'll revise it once more and send it out again."

Hustle can mean going out and creating a job that didn't exist. Gail Wells conceived an idea, detailed it in a proposal, took it to the publisher of the hometown weekly, and explained why she was the right person for the job. She got four! pages! a week! While a new shopping center was in early construction, an enterprising freelancer investigated and found out who the manager was, then went to see him. The writer went armed with a carefully detailed proposal. "I know you're going to put out an advertising insert prior to your opening, anyway," he said. He offered to compose quality articles featuring the businesses and personalities that will occupy the new center. He got the job and he did a good job.

You could do the same. You could present a workshop, class, or lecture. Contact the decision-makers at the community college, church, business, or civic group with your proposal.

Note "proposal." That's a specific plan, to an eyelash. Purpose, objectives, format, outline of content, when and how long, and for how much. If you need help with the proper bureaucratic formula for proposals, ask for the organization's form, or ask one of those masters of the process: a non-profit organization's grant writer or a special education teacher. (Okay, kids, this is a test. How many kinds of proposals have been discussed in this book? Name them and explain them.)

Serendipity For the hustling writer, serendipities are treasures under stones. But you have to stoop over and turn the stones; and then, the stones are for stepping.

> "Serendipities are all around out there," says R.G. Williscroft. But those gems don't fly through the window of your tower. If you would find a pearl, you must first go diving for oysters.

Very often one thing turns up something else more than you expected, taking you farther than you'd imagined. I sent to *The Humanist* a grim satire of the then-growing issue of sexism in language, and in the article I cited a book supporting a point. The rejection, a full-page non-boilerplate, explained that the topic was still painful among *Humanist's* staff; but would I send a review of the cited book. It led to assignments as a regular reviewer for a couple of years.

Conversely, I sent to another mag a review which they couldn't use, but how would I like to write some articles for them. A rejection isn't always a rejection.

When *West Side* newspaper was one issue old, I took a couple of pieces and a sheaf of proposals to the editor and told him I'd do three months or six pieces on trial, free. Next thing I knew I was "Regional Editor". Wow, I had a title and even a "column." And, gee, it took Erma Bombeck years to get her own column.

After a workshop I presented at Chemeketa Community College, a participant told me she had written an account of her autistic child, of his emergence from the shadows and of her own growth. When the youngster was an infant, the professional diagnosis was deaf, speechless, and retarded, with a prognosis of lifelong immobility and a recommendation of institutionalization. She refused to believe it, she would not let it be so.

The story piqued my interest because my youngest, though with a different condition, had at ten months been handed the same sentence. I, too, did not accept it, and neither did my daughter, who graduated valedictorian and earned her undergraduate degree two-tenths of a point short of honors. And I was interested, anyway, from a professional standpoint, having a master's in special education. (Most special ed teachers have compelling reasons, and believe it, those people really relate to those kids.)

I read the lady's manuscript. It was good. I liked it. Now it is *Winter's Flower: An Autistic Child* by Ranae Johnson, published in 1988 by Rickreall Creek House. Serendipities are reciprocal: they benefit both.

Well, this isn't supposed to be an autobiography. It is supposed to illustrate that it . . . can . . . be . . . done! This is the dumb third grader, remember, and the kid who damn near took a D on the freshman paper. This is to tell you: If I can . . . you can; believe you can.

Sometimes ya gots ta be pushy. A brassy fanfare is just another, more vivid, more dramatic version of a hustle. Be bold. If angels fear to tread, it means nobody else is there and you'll have the field to yourself.

Brass Quartet Let me tell you about a brassy quartet.

Pat Jossey, former editor of *Earthtone*, told a conference she knew she was violating all the rules when she walked into the magazine's office carrying 14 completed manuscripts and asked to see the editor. As it happened, *Earthtone* had no editor at the moment. Pat walked out with the job.

Eighteen years ago Jerry Easterling took a poem to the *Capital Journal* (now *Statesman-Journal*), which ordinarily used neither poetry nor freelance work. He's been there ever since.

A publisher, new and on a shoelace, prepared to produce a book about the livestock business. With brass enough to start a band, the press asked a feed manufacturing firm to "support the book", since the author is a dealer in their product. Brass enough for a $500 donation.

After a freelancer read a firm's promotional brochure, he sent a critique to the company's head honcho. This phrase is good, he wrote, this one ambiguous, this doesn't say what you mean, this passage means what you don't intend it to. "Your literature needs an editor," he concluded.

Well, the boss - man was either furious, curious, or impressed, because he invited his critic to come for a visit and a look-see. By the time the writer left, he'd been hired as an editor and thousands from their reciprocal serendipity.

Finally, brothers and sisters. (*Rustle and shuffle as congregation puts on shoes, clicks off stopwatches, snaps notebooks, searches for purses, fumbles coatsleeves.)*

Be gritty. Be okay or be conceited, whatever your generation calls the condition that enables you to disregard discouragement. Be steadfast in your belief in yourself and be unwilling to let 'em grind you down. And those youngsters - you can be that one personal influence in some young life that either builds or demolishes; either way you'll be remembered. Be remembered well.

Be hustley. Engage brain and move feet and DO it.

Be bold, be brazen, be brassy. Be innovative, be creative.

Be a writer.

CONFERENCE

DISPLAY AREA

Copyright Information

Cover Letter for Short Fiction

Cover Letter for Non-Fiction Article

Photo Release Form

Manuscript Preparation: Sample

Freebies!

Directories of Periodicals

Grammar Hot Lines

Products and Services

COPYRIGHT INFORMATION

From Copyright Basics Circular 1, Copyright Office,
Library of Congress, Washington D.C. 20559.
Copyright Office Hotline, (202) 287-9100

How to secure a copyright

"The way in which copyright is secured under the present law is frequently misunderstood. No publication or registration or other action in The Copyright Office is required to secure a copyright.

Under the present law, copyright is secured automatically when the work is created, and a work is "created" when it is fixed in a copy or phonorecord for the first time. In general, "copies" are material objects from which a work can be read or visually perceived either directly or with the aid of a machine or device, such as books, manuscripts, sheet music, film, videotape, or microfilm."

Under law, your work is automatically coprighted as soon as you commit it to videoscreen, paper, or disk from which the visual, written version of your material is retrievable. This also applies to sound recordings and to Braille on paper.

Form of Notice for Visually Perceptible Copies

Under law, your work is copyrighted when you write it. It's easy, fast, and free, however, to affix the notice on your work:

Symbol	© 1989 William S. Williams
Word	Copyright 1989 William S. Williams
Abbreviation	Copr. 1989 William S. Williams

What works are protected

- literary works
- dramatic works, including accompanying music
- musical works, including words
- pantomimes and choreographic works
- pictorial, graphic, and sculptural works
- motion pictures and other audiovisual works
- sound recordings

What is not protected by copyright

These categories of material are not eligible:

"Works that have not been fixed in a tangible form of expression. For example, choreographic works that have not been notated or recorded, or improvisational speeches or performances that have not been written or recorded.

Titles, names, short phrases, slogans; familiar symbols or designs; mere listings of ingredients or contents.

Ideas, procedures, methods, systems, processes, concepts, principles, discoveries, or devices, as distinguished from a description, explanation, or illustration.

Works consisting entirely of information that is common property and containing no original authorship. For example, standard calendars, height and weight charts, tape measures and rules, and lists or tables taken from public documents or other common sources.

Works produced, published, and distributed by the United States Government"

Note **ideas** are not covered by copyright until they are set down in written or sound recorded form. To tell someone your story idea does not copyright the idea; to outline or summarize the story copyrights the **words you write.**

How to Register your Copyright

Send the following three elements together in the same envelope or package to Register of Copyrights, Copyright Office, Library of Congress, Washington D.C. 20559:

1. A properly completed application form

2. A nonrefundable filing fee of $10 for each application

3.A nonreturnable deposit of the work being registered:
If the work is unpublished, one complete copy
If the work was first published in the United States on or after January 1, 1978, two complete copies or phonorecords of the best edition.

Unpublished Collections

Your work may be registered in unpublished form as a "collection" with one application and one fee. This applies to a complete book manuscript or parts thereof; music, poetry, a single audio or videotape or several as a single collection. You may gather all your unpublished workand register everything you've written for one single $10 fee, under the following conditions:

"The elements of the collection are assembled in an orderly form;
The combined elements bear a single title identifying the collection as a whole;
The copyright claimant in all the elements and in the collection as a whole is the same; and
All the elements are by the same author, or, if they are by different authors, at least one of the authors has contributed copyrightable authorship to each element.

"Unpublished collections are indexed in the Catalog of *Copyright Entries* only under the collection titles."

Application Forms

To obtain your registration forms, write the Copyright Office and request the appropriate form as follows:

Form TX: for published and unpublished non-dramatic literary works

Form SE: for serials, newspapers, magazines, any form of periodicals issued in succession bearing numerical or chronological designations

Form PA: for published and unpubublished works of the performing arts, including music, drama, dance, pantomimes, audiovisual works.

Form VA: for published and unpublished works of the visual arts, pictorial, graphic, sculptural

Form SR: for published and unpublished sound recordings

COVER LETTER TO ACCOMPANY SHORT FICTION

Your address

Their address

Dear Editor or Editor's Name:

"Cobblestones" is original unpublished fiction not previously submitted to any other publication. The story is fiction and the characters and their names are fictitious; any resemblance to real persons or situations is unintentional.

I offer to Your Magazine first rights. If accepted, the story will not be offered or sold to any other publication in Your Magazine's readership area for a period of one year, or for such time as you specify. I certify that the work is entirely my own in concept, content, and composition, and that no portion has been borrowed, adapted, or quoted from any source published or unpublished.

Mariloo Bentley

Mariloo Bentley/ *Check goes to this name*
Mary Bender *Bentley's pseudonymn: This will be name on story's byline*

BIONOTE:

Mary Bender waits tables at a West Village dinner house and writes from her home in East Hamlet, Montana. This is Bender's six hundredth contribution to Your Magazine.

Most publications request short bionotes; Bentley includes hers with the submission .

Permission is granted for copying any portion or substance of this page.

COVER LETTER FOR NON-FICTION MANUSCRIPT

Your address

Their address

Dear Editor or Editor's Name:

In response to your go-ahead, I have prepared "Alzheimers: New Hope for Families". Your suggested changes have been incorporated and it's a substantially stronger piece than the one I originally proposed.

Individual resource persons are credited and quoted within the body of the text. Except for passages cited, the piece is entirely my own and no portion of the text has been copied, borrowed, adapted, or quoted from any source other than the individuals credited. A listing of resources is attached, together with addresses, titles, and phone numbers for your records and verification.

I certify that this article is original and unpublished and that it is an exclusive submission for Rag Mag.

Joel MacAdam

Enclosures:

Manuscript
Photos (5) w/captions
Photo Release Forms
List of Resource Persons
SASE

BIONOTE:

Joel MacAdam is a certified physical therapist and a freelance writer. He lives in Shortview, Idaho with his wife and six grandchildren. MacAdam's 72-year-old mother, an Alzheimer's victim, lives with them.

PHOTO RELEASE FORM

Nearly every publication requires a photo release to accompany any photograph in which the subject is identifiable. Its purpose is legal protection for the publication and for you.

Commercially prepared release forms are available. They include the words, "In consideration for renumeration received", and that strongly implies author will pay subject, and that may not be so good for the author if the photo is for a spec article. Also, some commercially prepared release forms say "For use in (title of article) to appear in (publication); and that's not so good, either, if it's a spec article, or if you'll be using the photo again in a subsequent "spoked" piece.

The simple form below is practical, many purpose, and noncommittal.

PERMISSION TO USE PHOTOGRAPH

I hereby give my permission to ______________________________

(author's name)

to use my photograph in article (s) for publication.

Signature ______________________________

Address ______________________________

Telephone ______________________________

Permission is granted for copying this form.

Susan Henry
2519 E. Ellendale
Dallas, OR 97338
(503) 623-6889

Approx. 1200 words
One-time Rights

Copyright 1988 S. Henry

*In manuscript preparation,
the packaging is as important
as the product . . . appearance
is everything.*

MANUSCRIPT PREPARATION:

A SAMPLE

By T. R. O'Schmidtmeyer

For that final last-draft copy you prepare for submission, the packaging is as important as the product. If it isn't formatted correctly, many editors won't read it. Appearance is everything.

"Look at this," the editor of a monthly told me, holding a page of single-spaced type with no address, no margins. "This guy is either a greenhorn or a maverick. Why can't I attract the pros?"

"Judging from the submissions I receive, what writers need most is a course in manuscript preparation," said Anne Grimm-Richardson of tiptoe publishing (no caps). That's why at tiptoe's Wilderness Writer's Conference, Ann scheduled "Manuscript Preparation" first, even before the Keynote (Robert M. Pyle, "Getting the Words Right"). Package . . . Product.

Materials: 8½ x 11" white typing paper, 20# weight. Avoid ripple or woven textures as too ostentatious. Do not use lightweights such as the variety store "200 sheets for $1.29" packages. Do not, no, never, use erasable.

Ribbon: Fresh-looking. Type can be black or it can be dark black. Not grey.

Type: First, pica, or at least 12-pitch. Now, no editors told me they'd actually refuse to read elite type. . . But if it were close to a tossup between a pica piece and an elite . . .

Secondly, type style. Preferred are the old traditional Establishment typefaces, fonts, or style--no individualistic stuff. Clear, clean letters, produced on a clean element, wheel, or keys. If yours is a cherished old faithful friend of a manual portable that reproduces light-toned letters with filled-in e's and

(more)

a's, well, your copy doesn't look good; the page is not the "clean copy" editors specify. When I said this to a workshop, an elderly gentleman was very affronted. "My old Royal portable with the sticking keys has done me well for thirty-five years," he said in hurt tones. And, gee, I don't know what to say but that it doesn't look good, and appearance is everything.

This is manuscript format. Your Conference Welcome is in manuscript format. These are the showing. Now the telling. . .

Margins: 1½" on all sides. That's a lot of white space. This is not the time to conserve paper. Right-hand margin: unjustified. Remember "ragged right."

Using a bold black felt marker, you can make a backing sheet with margins measured. Just type within the outline. That's especially handy for right margins and last line of the page.

In former times it was considered correct to hyphenate at the end of a line if you observed proper syllabication. That's no longer the rule, thanks to word processing technoquirk. Do not divide words at endline. Exception: It's okay to hyphenate words that are correctly spelled with a hyphen. You can type "even-tempered", which is hyphenated anyway; but not "even-tem-

(more)

pered".

First page: One inch from the top, upper left, your real name (the person who gets the check), address, phone number, single-spaced. In the upper right, approximate word count, the rights you are selling, and notice of copyright if you wish.

Half to two-thirds down: The title, somewhat centered, in caps. This leaves a lot of white space, and if that's counter to your frugal nature, fight it. This is not the time to conserve paper.

If you write a "blurb" or "hook" for the piece, place it about halfway between phone number and title.

Double-spaced below the title: The name to appear on the byline. Your Social Security/IRS/FBI/church pledge name is in the upper left; your pen name is below the title.

Double- or triple-spaced below byline: Begin text. Type six lines on first page.

Do not paginate (page number) first page.

Subsequent pages: About 3/4 inch or 3 spaces from top of the page, a "header" in either of two formats.

A. Williams: Abbreviated title/2

B. Williams: Abbreviated title 2

For a multiple-chapter work, a 2-line header:

(more)

Henry/O'Schmidtmeyer: Ms prep/5

Williams: Plastic spurs *(cumulative page of text)* 9867
Chapt 450/85 *(chapter, page of chapter)*

Begin text three spaces down from header, or on the line showing through on the backing page you've measured.

Lines per page: Some manuals prescribe 25 lines of type per page, although one specifies 21. Be consistent. Exception: Do not leave a final page with only one line. Either compose the last page with 26 lines, or type 24 lines on the next-to-the-last so the final page has two or more lines.

Word count, called for in upper right, page 1: To allocate space and plan page layout, the editor needs to know how many words you've written. Count the words in a few lines of a few pages--say four lines on four different pages--and compute the average words-per-line. Multiply the number of lines of text by the average words per line.

Example

4 full pp @ 25 lines = 100 lines
+ first p 6 lines
+ last p 9 lines
Total text 115 lines

Average words/line 9.5

115 x 9.5 = 1092.5 / Approx. 1100 words

(I round off to nearest 25 words)

(more)

Count all words. (A, and, the occupy space, too.)

Hyphenated words: Count each. "Going-to-be writer" takes the space of 4 words.

Qualifier: Some publications who pay by the word consider hyphenateds a single word. I go ahead and count them all. I've received by-the-word payments that didn't tally according to the words actually printed, anyway. In the last analysis, I think, the word count is what the editor says it is. Don't agonize it.

Rights, upper right, first page: Publishers buy the right to publish your work. "First rights" are for the first time the work is published; "Second" or "second serial" is for previously published pieces. When you offer serial rights, be absolutely certain that the first publication did not buy "all rights", which means you no longer own the work. Likewise, some publishers assume ownership of copyright, in which case the item is no longer yours to sell.

Many, many periodicals state they buy "One-time Rights". I like that nice general, non-entangling term, and I offer one-timers a lot. If that isn't okay with the publication, they'll say so.

On the bottom of each page except the last, you can indicate the piece is continued. Below the last line, type

(more) or -more-

It's centered, 2 or 3 spaces below the last line of text--that will be in the margin. Some instructions tell you to do this; others don't mention it. If in doubt, do.

On the last page, you can indicate completion. Three or four spaces below the last line, type - End - or (The End), or, if your roots are in journalism, -30-. Or, you can do this to show you're through telling:

#########

BIONOTE: The author, a former teacher, lives on a farm near Dallas, Oregon with her husband, a former teacher, where she freelances and he raises Black Angus and Black Baldies.

Most magazines and very few newspapers request a short "bioblurb" to tag your articles. I usually affix one in this way; they can use it or pitch it. This also serves as the "About The Author" appended to most books, and which I'm told should be included. . . so here it is. Anything else that makes any difference is incorporated somewhere within the text, anyway.

FREEBIES!!!

"Guidelines for Nonsexist Use of Language". SASE to NCTE, 111 Kenyon Rd., Urbana IL 61801

"Publishing Poynters". Dan Poynter, Para Publishing, PO Box 4232, Santa Barbara, CA 94109

"Northwest Literary Arts Calendar". Not sent to individuals, but can be requested by libraries, writers' groups. Michael Polacek, Oregon Arts Commission, 835 Summer Street, Salem, OR 97371

"Phone Area Codes". All area codes listed in numerical order gives location, time zone. SASE to Peggy Glenn, Aames - Allen Publishing, 1106 Main St., Huntington Beach, CA 92684

"Writers Northwest Newsletter". Quarterly with articles, marketing updates, new publications, products. Media Weavers, Rt. 3 Box 376, Hillsboro, OR 97214

RESOURCE DIRECTORIES FROM COLLEGES. Postpaid. Send post card or call. Penn State Contacts, Pennsylvania State University, 312 Old Main, University Park, PA 16802. 814-856-7517

University of California, Irvine, Media Guide, UCI Communications Office, 6 Floor Ad Bldg, U Cal, Irvine, CA 92717. 714-856-9622

George Washington University Media Guide, GW News Service, 705 Gelman Library, Washington DC 20057. 202-994-6460

Georgetown University Press Contacts, Robin S. Payes, Director of News and Special Projects, 37th & O Sts. N.W., Washington DC 20057. 202-625-4151

Vanderbilt Sources Handbook, Vanderbilt Univ, News & Public Affairs, 511 KirklandHall, Nashville TN 37240. 615-322-2706

Purdue Contacts, Office of University Relations, Purdue Univ, West Lafayette, IN 47907. 317-494-2096

ZIP Code inquiries: Give street address, city, state. They'll tell you the correct ZIP. From USPS. 1-800-228-8777. 7:30 a.m. 8:00 p.m. EDT

US Copyright Office 24hour hotline. Call and leave a message for application forms to be sent you. 202-287-9100

DIRECTORIES OF PERIODICALS

WRITER'S MARKET and LITERARY MARKETPLACE, although the best-known listings of periodicals and publications, are by no means the most definitive. Those directories list the best-known *paying* markets. . . and you already know there are many good reasons for being published in non-paying media.

The following are available in mid-size-and-larger libraries, and smaller libraries can obtain them for you on inter-library loan. Each lists hundreds and skousands (literally translated "skillions--well, a couple thousand, anyway") of "little" and literary magazines, professional, limited interest, in-house, outhouse, poetry, so on.

AYER DIRECTORY OF PUBLICATIONS. IMS Press/IMS Communications Inc. Lists periodicals published in U.S., Canada, Republic of Philippines, Bermuda, Bahamas. By state; within states, by city. Indexed also by classification: Magazines of general circulation; fraternal; college; agricultural; Black; Jewish; religious; newsletters; newspapers.

ULRICH'S INTERNATIONAL PERIODICALS DIRECTORY. R. R. Bowker. Mags by subject.

WORKING PRESS OF THE NATION SERIES. National Research Bureau, Inc.
Vol. 1: Newspaper Directory   Vol. 2: Magazine Directory

STANDARD PERIODICALS DIRECTORY. Oxbridge Communications. Carries more listings, organization makes material more easily findable than above listings. Indicates publications accepting freelance work, payment schedules.

INTERNATIONAL DIRECTORY OF LITTLE MAGAZINES AND SMALL PRESSES. Dustbooks. Annual.

DIRECTORY OF POETRY PUBLISHERS. Dustbooks. Annual.

AMERICAN HUMANITIES INDEX. Whitson Publishing Co. Indexes about 300 small circulation literary magazines, indexed by author, subject.

DIRECTORY OF LITERARY MAGAZINES. Coordinating Council of Literary Magazines, New York.

THE WRITER'S YELLOW PAGES. Steve Davis Publishing. Lists every imaginable facet of writing, producing, publishing, promoting, peddling. Name, address, phone number of over 5000 magazines. If you are self-publishing, you really need this listing of . . . everything. But! It's only a list, nothing more. $19.95 from P.O. Box 190831, Dallas, TX 75219.

GRAMMAR HOTLINES

Don't leave it split, dangling, or misplaced. And don't count on an editor to catch and correct; if there are too many errors, most editors would rather return than revise.

Grammar hotlines require no fee; and they claim they haven't been stumped yet.

Since these lines are stationed at colleges and universities, they are likely to be closed during break periods between terms. Here are some with the most steady hours. A much longer listing of grammar lines appears in *The Writer's Yellow Pages*, Steve Davis Publishing Company.

GRAMMAR HOTLINE, MOORPORK COLLEGE, Moorpark, CA. 805/529-2321.
8 a.m. - 12 M PST, Mon-Fri

GRAMMARPHONE, FROSTBURG STATE COLLEGE, Frostburg, MD. Call collect!
301/689-4327. 10 a.m. - 12 M EST, Mon-Fri

GRAMMARPHONE, TRITON COLLEGE, River Grove, IL. 312/456-0300 Ext. 254.
8:30 a.m. - 9 p.m. CST Mon-Thur; 10 am - 1 pm Sat

LEARNING LINE, SAN ANTONIO COLLEGE, San Antonio, TX 78284.
512/733-2503. 8 a.m. - 9:45 p.m. CST Mon-Thur; 8 a.m. - 4 p.m. Fri

DIAL-A-GRAMMAR, RAYMOND WALTERS COLLEGE, Cincinnati, OH.
513/745-4312. Tapes requests; returns answer via collect call. (You pay for two phone calls; but you can ask your questions at those strange hours writers work.

# # # # #

DIRECTORY OF EXPERTS, AUTHORITIES, & SPOKESPERSONS

"The Talk Show Guest Directory"

Here's a source of resource persons for writers and journalists! 3,569 sources indexed by 5,378 topics. Listings by both topic and by individuals /organizations.

Individuals listed have ASKED to be there; the publisher includes reporting forms so users can keep the editor advised as to effectiveness of persons listed.

Guarantee: Phone numbers that work, people who say yes.

AND a free subscriber newsletter reviews the best sources, provides you with interview comments and ideas. You can use these ideas to plan the interviews you will be having when your book comes out . . .And you'll receive information as to how you can be listed yourself in this directory, free, so that you will be called for talk show interviews.

ORDER FROM: Mitchell P. Davis, Broadcast Interview Source, 2500 Wisconsin Avenue N.W., Washington DC 20007. 202/3334904. It's $25 postpaid. A bargain if you're a writer needing authoritative information or an author needing some free air time.

MANUSCRIPTS INTERNATIONAL ESP (Editing for Small Presses)

Professional editing for a professionally polished book manuscript. ESP editors are experienced, weathered, water tested pros, thoroughly schooled in grammar, composition, and structure.

Specialty: Book manuscripts for small and independent presses and self - publishers. Bluepencil editing (it's really a red pen, guys) or further refinement as you need and as you direct. They promise professionalism at a writer's price.

MI ESP, 408 E. Main, Dayton, WA 99328. 509-382-2436

PHOENIX INFORMATION SERVICES connects writers with editors through a database network which cross references member writers and their work with current requests from editors. Membership includes on-file information about articles writers have completed and/or queries; a Writer's Profile, made available to editors seeking writers with specific qualifications for certain assignments; evaluation of marketability of work; an information network about members; a toll-free answer line to answer questions about writing and marketing and to provide daily updates of editors' needs; and a newsletter. Membership $130/year. Phoenix Writer's Service, 57 Main Street, S.H. 8119, Littlefork, MN 56653. 1-800-548-3725.

I have to add that once you get into Phoenix's system, which is kind of a hoop-jump because it understands only those fill-ins you perform with a soft #2 pencil, it works. Moments after becoming a member, I called them, and , on their own nickel, they told me of four different editor requests just received - two were publications so new they weren't yet in writers' mags' market updates. The same day, I had three pieces off, thanks to their information. (Repeat: Don't pitch out stuff you've already written!)

INDEX

FROM RICKREALL CREEK HOUSE

Box 13 Rickreall, Oregon 97371 (503) 623-6889

CATTLE ANNIE

By Ann Frey Cummins. Foreword by Jerry Easterling, illus by Jack Corbet and Rachelle Powell. 184 pp, paper. Appendix. EAN/Bookland bar coded. $9.95

ISBN 943149-04-5 CIP 87-062832

A cattlecar load of cow tales, mostly side-achers, mostly not too embellished, about critters and folks in the farm and stock trade . . . and earthy philosphies and practical information for everyone of the rural persuasion. Recipient of Manna Pro Company award for contribution to stock husbandry. 1988's best seller at Northwest stock auctions.

A WRITER IS A STATE OF BEING: YOUR PERSONAL DESKTOP CONFERENCE

By Susan Henry. Illus by Jack Corbett. 8 1/2 x 11 perfect bound paperback. Appendix, Index. EAN/Bookland bar coded. $12.95

ISBN 0-943149-05-3 CIP 87-51002

A writer's conference-at-home, featuring comments, tips, how-to's from scores of editors, agents, publishers, writers, poets, authors, journalists. Samples, examples, forms, formats, sources, resources, freebies, names and addresses . . . and observations on the state of being a writer - and debunking the old mythologies.

I WANT A DOBERMAN BY MY DESK:
Other Stuff You Learn At School
Susan Henry. 122 pp, paperback.
$7.95. ISBN 0-939169-00-2
CIP 85-50548

With cheerful barbed humor, a veteran teacher conducts a readers' tour of your kids' Alma Marmee. Nominated for 1987 Pushcart Prize for small press selections. Give a copy to a teacher you like . . . or to one you don't.

COUNTRY CHAFF II

Jerry Easterling. Illustrated by Kristi Gilman. 144 pp, paper. $6.95
ISBN 0-944540-03-1 CIP 87-51280

A celebration of life in tender, muscular, humorous, poignant vignettes from one of Oregon's finest writers. The opening selection won the 1987 Gannett Prize, designating Easterling the outstanding writer of Gannett journalists.

ORDER FORM FOR RICKREALL CREEK HOUSE BOOKS

SAN 668-1166

STOPs - yes

Quantity	Title	Price	Total
	CATTLE ANNIE	$9.95	
	A WRITER IS A STATE OF BEING: Your Personal Desktop Conference	12.95	
	I WANT A DOBERMAN BY MY DESK Other Stuff You Learn At School	7.95	
	COUNTRY CHAFF	6.95	

Postage: $1.25 for one book;

Two or more 90¢ each $______

Total $______

MasterCard VISA ______

Schools and libraries: Enclose P.O.

All other orders, remit with order

Exp Date ______

To

Cardholder Signature ______

RICKREALL CREEK HOUSE
BOX 13
Rickreall, OR 97371

SHIP TO ______